Praise

Maintaining® Greatness

Understanding that you are necessary and created for greatness is one thing. However, having the privilege of uncovering the formula and method of maintaining greatness, now that is a "life gift" that creates a ripple effect! Grayson Marshall is a brilliant mind that understands that greatness is both observed and demonstrated. You now have the wisdom to be greater in your hands and you get to choose your next big move. Be Amazing!
-Kyra R. Hardwick, MBA – Imagine Excellence

Towering above the chaotic sea of self-help hysteria and superficial hype, Grayson Marshall offers a no-nonsense message that immediately shifts the way you think and the choices that you make. As both a leadership professor and business/life coach, I consider this a must-read for each of my students/clients. An empowering piece of work! *Maintaining Greatness* will be one of my go-to coaching tools from now on.
-Dr. Kimberly Bynum

Grayson is wholeheartedly dedicated to serving people, building them up and leading them, by example, on the path to identifying and pursuing their unique purpose and fulfilling their God-designed destiny. He truly is the Metacognition Expert and *M.A.I.N.T.A.I.N.I.N.G. Greatness* is a step-by-step playbook, teaching you how to align your thoughts with consistent action and a spirit of excellence, create and sustain positive change and live the life you've always imagined. Think of him as your personal Gr(ay)tness Coach!
-Lashantah Holliday, Educator/Entrepreneur

Grayson Marshall Jr.

MAINTAINING GREATNESS

Managing your gifts for limitless living

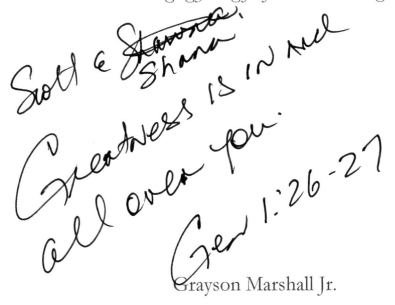

Scott & ~~Tamara~~ Shana,
Greatness is in and all over you.
Gen 1:26-27

Grayson Marshall Jr.

Foreword by Les Brown

Grayson

From Scott Falany
12/5/2019

ISBN-13: 978-0-692-19562-8

Page composition, content development & interior designed by Rackhouse Publishing

Scriptures marked (NASB) are retrieved from the new American standard Bible

For information about custom editions, special sales, premium and corporate purchases, please contact Grayson Marshall Jr. via email:
Grayson@graysonmarshalljr.com

First Edition
Printed in the U.S.A

This book is dedicated to my deceased parents Grayson B. Marshall Sr. and Marie Celine Howell Marshall and the lineage in both family lines. I came from an "always do your best" environment. They wanted what was best for me and showed me a way to pursue it. They did not, however, teach me how to MAINTAIN and with this book I am honored to finish what they started and share it with everyone who also wants to have that life.

Grayson Marshall Jr.

Contents

ACKNOWLEDGMENTS

There are so many people I would like to thank in this book. First God for the inspiration and desire from the heart to see this through to completion.

To my sister Terri Lynn who has my biggest fan and support system.

Thank you Dr. Adrian A Gentry and Jason Oliver for being the iron that sharpens this iron.

Thanks to the most amazing content format & review specialist and subject matter director anyone could ever ask for. Melynda Rackley you have been a Godsend to me.

To the men of ADAM, there is nothing better than accountability and you provide that for me and I am so grateful for it.

Patrick Cowherd thank you for being a sounding board and a reminder of the path I am pursuing and the responsibility that come with it.

Dr. Kim Bynum you are the support that has made all of this come to pass.

To the "ITBEW" family Angel Mills, Jacklyn Parker Fann Jessica Glover, Charistina Popovick, James Watkins, Richard Hunter, Amy Caldwell, Jessica Wilkerson, Edwina Wilkerson, Christine Alley, Jasmine Souers, Michellita Taylor you are the best people to have in a tribe.

Will Prude for being a friend & Cisco Turpin for being the voice of reason in my life.

Tiffany "TJ" Deserve for being so positive and teaching greatness to so many. Candice Smithman for all of your spiritual support and guidance & Glenn Ellison for your commitment to the greatness for the next generation.

To the incomparable Leslie "Les" Calvin Brown for all of your belief and support.

To every coach, teacher, mentor, pastor, and leader who is charged with the task of empowerment and improvement, and everyone who has allowed toe privilege to share this message with you or your group. I thank you.

To my kids and grandkids that I want to see become great and maintain it, I appreciate you. And to Darlene, thank you as well.

FOREWORD

My name is Les Brown. It has been said that these are the best of times and the worst of times. Here, Grayson Marshall, gifted author, powerful speaker, and coach offers a book that gives you the methods and strategies to carve a tunnel of hope through the mountains of despair, stress and distractions that many people are experiencing today.

You have something special. You have greatness in you. To find it, each chapter lays out a step-by-step process on how to keep your head up during down times. Get ready for a journey that takes you beyond motivation and positive thinking. You can set up camp with what he teaches you because of creation's vast knowledge passion and determination to create major breakthroughs with his speeches workshops and writings. I can assure you by the time you complete this book you will live your life at a new and more powerful level.

Tom Hanks' character in the movie Forrest Gump said, "life is like a box of chocolates you never know what you're going to get." In other words, life can catch us on "The Blind Side". Well this book gives you a ladder that allows you to climb out of the dungeons of despair and darkness to bask in the brightness of a better place where the sun always shines – that's your something special.

Grayson teaches you how to use your inner power and

presence, living from the inside out. In other words, it doesn't matter what happens TO you; what matters most is what happens IN you. He provides the tools to cultivate your inner greatness and maintain it because when you're pursuing your greatness you are more apt to behave in a limitless way. I call Grayson a power brother whom I admire. I hold him in high regard and encourage everyone to read this book. It will change lives. That's my story and I'm sticking with it.

1

MASTERING THE MIND
UNPACK, UNDERSTAND & REBUILD

*You are who you create yourself to be and all that occurs in your life is
the result of your own making.*
-Stephen Richards

Mastering The Mind

Where does all imagination begin? Where do we develop urges and ideas before they become actions? It is almost implausible to clutch the reality that a small three pound organ controls it all. The internal control unit, also known as the brain, is the most fascinating and important component to mastering the mind. If we want to maintain greatness then the first thing that we need to do is master the mindset that it takes to be great. Simply put, we must reframe our thoughts and to do that we must first get an understanding of how they work. The current and ongoing challenge during the journey to mind mastery is figuratively rebuilding our brains. I often wonder if we really understand the power of and within the internal control unit. Perhaps if we were fully aware of its ability we would indubitably engage in the process of reconstruction. Now, I must warn you that this process requires intense evaluation. So, let's make an agreement to be acquiescent with ourselves as we uncover the channels of our brain that allow us to master the mind.

Mind mastery is the necessary base for maintaining greatness. When we talk about mastering the mindset we are talking about acquiring knowledge, understanding, skill and technique to actively and consistently grow in relation to the psyche. Before we move forward it's important to understand the literal job and main parts of the brain. As we all may know the overall job of the brain is to control all of the functions within the body. It receives and interprets all information from our five senses while personifying the foundation of our mind and soul. This is no easy task and is only accomplished through the exquisite composition and interworking of the cerebrum, cerebellum and brain stem.

Mastery is a term used to infer procedural growth in the evolutionary understanding of how things work. While the mind refers to the interconnectivity of our thoughts. The mind, in and of itself, is the critical component to creating the life that we have always imagined. The thinking process is one that often goes unchecked or unevaluated because we have stopped actively thinking for ourselves. As a society, we tend to rely on the thoughts and influences of other people more than discovering or developing our own. Thus, since we don't think for ourselves, we don't really understand our thinking or how our thinking totally affects the life we create. Ultimately, if we are going to get to the root of mastering our mindset, we have to go back to the beginning where it all started and reclaim our birth right. Our initial birth right was to think for ourselves. It was to be in control of our thoughts and actions and have dominion over everything that God created as was commanded in Genesis 1:24-31.

26 Then God said, "Let Us make man in Our image, according to

Our likeness; and let them rule over the fish of the sea and over the birds of the sky and over the cattle and over all the earth, and over every creeping thing that creeps on the earth." 27 God created man in His own image, in the image of God He created him; male and female He created them. 28 God blessed them; and God said to them, "Be fruitful and multiply, and fill the earth, and subdue it; and rule over the fish of the sea and over the birds of the sky and over every living thing that moves on the earth." 29 Then God said, "Behold, I have given you every plant yielding seed that is on the surface of all the earth, and every tree which has fruit yielding seed; it shall be food for you; 30 and to every beast of the earth and to every bird of the sky and to everything that moves on the earth which has life, I have given every green plant for food"; and it was so. 31 God saw all that He had made, and behold, it was very good. (NASB)

UNPACK

Imagine being trapped in the bottom of a box full of all of the negative ideas that have now attached to your consciousness. Standing in the center you look around with blurred and limited vision. You notice the broken expectations being held up by self imposed stereo types. To the right you see all the societal statistics, while the left exposes tainted religious belief systems mirroring your habits on the wall. In all of your limited evaluation you discover that there is a staircase just 6 feet away, but you are separated by the barrier of all the lies living in your conscious mind. The only way out is to remove the barrier, and the only way to remove the barrier is to recognize and eliminate deception.

Greatness has always and will always be within us, it is our responsibility to continuously unpack the thoughts and actions that serve as a barrier to maintaining it . The barrier isn't built in a day or an hour, it starts with a small statement, an unintentional act or unforgettable experience that sits inside waiting to be nurtured for growth. One thing I know for sure is that deception within the conscious or subconscious mind is powerful and, no matter how small the seed once planted, it can take a lifetime to uproot.

To get a deeper level of understanding we must be aware that the mind is made up of two designated compartments –the conscious and subconscious mind. While the two coexist in the mind one is significantly more dominant than the other. The conscious mind reveals our rational awareness while the subconscious mind conceals the layer of influential awareness.

I was six years old when I experienced internalized racism, light skin was "in" and my tint was to dark. As a child I learned to dislike my skin from those who looked just like me. Time moved on but my mind held on to the banter of my peers who shamed me for my midnight skin. Unintentionally, over time I nurtured this idea and, before I knew it, my box was full of insecurities, combined with the conscious desire to be accepted by those who could not see beyond what society had placed in their minds. If we are honest with ourselves, we may realize that at some point our capacity to think freely is masked at some point or another by unconscious programming. Until we uncover that very central part of our being, maintaining greatness is somewhat out of reach.

In an effort to cope with my growing self hate I immersed myself into athletics. I became a stellar athlete; I was respected but never accepted. I constantly looked for a tribe to call my own because of the rejection from my own. I had an amazing work ethic as an athlete but no real understanding of my subconscious ability to tap into my greatness. I allowed everyone around me to think for me because I wanted their validation and it became my comfort zone. Once you get lost in someone else's thoughts they may began to control the way that you think. Unintentionally you succumb to their belief system or label about who you are. Without understanding of the subconscious mind one will always search for greatness outside of themselves. This lack of confidence, trust and ultimately lack of love are all due to the fact that we don't understand who we are or how to reclaim our birth right. Knowing how the mind works, helps us to self-adjust when information or concepts arise that challenge this new understanding we are attempting to build.

The conscious mind is the foundation of beliefs that are there to protect you. What becomes familiar becomes safe; what becomes safe becomes comfortable; and what becomes comfortable is where you want to spend more of your time. The subconscious mind is naturally much stronger than the conscious mind because it exist in a fear-free zone. It is also where all involuntary processes are housed –circulation, heartbeat, breathing and all biological requirements are synchronized within it. This is where the foundation of greatness lives and operates. However, if seeds of doubt and fear are planted, watered, and nourished there, that is what will grow.

For example, the subconscious mind may present a layer of fear as protection which then make fear become more important than walking by faith. Adopting this belief into the conscious mind ultimately leads to misunderstanding. This is why metacognition is so important. Metacognition by definition is the understanding and awareness of how you think, beginning with the acquisition of knowledge. For me the battle with self hate ended once I applied the knowledge of my birthright – thinking for myself. As I unpacked the barriers related to my skin color for instance, I began to unlock my subconscious mind. I no longer denied myself the right to think independently or be unapologetically great inside of my midnight skin. Unpacking opened the gate and allowed me to walk out of deception and into the greatness.

Lets revisit the box metaphor again. In a situation where

we feel trapped, our first, involuntary and most natural reaction is to scream out for help. This is because tend to focus more on the conscious mind –the less powerful of the two components of our thinking. The conscious mind says its rational to panic and frantically shuffle through the clutter. While the subconscious mind may lean a bit more towards using the clutter to climb over the barriers or meticulously uncover the way out. The subconscious mind recognizes the greatness but cannot force its influence onto the will of our consciousness.

Often times we fuel our actions from energy retrieved by a very restricted contributor to the mind. Before releasing the internalized racism, I thrived on a path cluttered with people and things that fed my insecurity. I believed that this was my way into acceptance, popularity and success. When we border our greatness with this limited source of consciousness we may become frustrated with the lack of results.

The conscious part of us can only do a little at a time, representing only about 5 percent of our mental capacity. Your greatness is not in the 5 percent. Our subconscious mind is so powerful and versatile yet we don't notice it controls 95 percent of our mental processes. Once we yield to the wonder of the subconscious mind we can unpack the learned limits which conceal greatness. In the conscious mind, the focus is action and will power; which, in the end, proves to be no match for the more influential subconscious mind.

So, now that we are unpacked, we are aware the challenge has transitioned from acquiring knowledge to applying it. In this case application requires rebuilding the mind to sow good seeds for an abundant harvest just as Galatians 6:7-9 admonishes:

> *7 Do not be deceived, God is not mocked; for whatever a man sows, this he will also reap. 8 For the one who sows to his own flesh will from the flesh reap corruption, but the one who sows to the Spirit will from the Spirit reap eternal life. 9 Let us not lose heart in doing good, for in due time we will reap if we do not grow weary.*
> *Galatians 6:7*

UNDERSTAND & REBUID

The ideas of my skin being too dark and not feeling good enough still lay dormant in my mind, but I now understand the power of my 95 percent –my subconscious. Once I completed my preliminary self-evaluations and adopted my personal realization of greatness, I had to change. It wasn't until my mid thirties that I began to flirt with the idea of rebuilding my thinking. It wasn't until my baptism at the age of 41 that I began to tackle the building journey. During my rebuilding process my mind was challenged on every side. I had to take ownership of my mind to understand and rebuild the ideas that had become a part of my identity. My faith in God's love laid a foundation for me to dive into the unknown. One imperative step to mastering the mind is accepting and owning where you are today, without excuses or explanations. The Bible says in John

8:32, *"You will know the truth and the truth will make you free."*

Owning it in your mind means acknowledging that the truth is here and making the conscious decision to be with your truth. Ownership allows one to take responsibility for any situation, thought or emotion. Greatness relies heavily on the act of ownership because it is tied to acceptance. If an individual is aware and fully owns a task, action or situation they know they have what it takes to overcome it. They know the access that they have to grace because they were born great, and they embrace the responsibility of owning where they are each day. The concept of ownership of the mind is vital because it doesn't allow for what plagued you in the past to be where you go for scrutiny and safety. It allows you to become the greatness that you are because "Greater is he that is in you than he that is in the world" (1 John 4:4).

Ultimately, when we can stand on truth, knowing what is in us, and when we can begin to make that our mantra, we reclaim our birth right. We were made in His image and His likeness even before inception. We were given the keys to the kingdom and given the authority to own it. Ownership becomes the key component to mastering the mind. The owning is where you are going to lift your vibration frequency; owning allows whatever happens in your life to be turned over to grace. When we engage in the act of ownership we remove the control of someone else over our life and restore it back to ourselves. It also important to own with understanding. Allowing the two to work together is what helps in maintaining greatness.

As we grow alongside technology, the amount of knowledge we have access to grows. However, what is missing is understanding. That is why in Psalm 4:7 we are admonished to not only get wisdom, but to also get understanding. Often times when we experience life without understanding, we are not aware of why we do the things that we do, act the way we act, or say the things we say. As a result of this lack of understanding the world has decided to put labels on our behaviors in an attempt to help us. These labels come in the form of diagnoses like schizophrenia, bipolar syndrome, social anxiety disorder and every other term for mental disorders. We have been led to believe that those labels are true representations of our identity. While it is true that those things have an impact on us, what we don't understand is that through reinforcing the labels we turned over our ability to own, understand and create a better mind. I believe we become whatever we are labeled. Thus, the more we embrace the labels we were not born with, the further we drift in the opposite direction of our birthright. An example of this would be the typical AA meeting, the individual stands and first says their birth name followed by a label. This label reminds them of the issue that has removed them from the purity of their name. When the alcoholic states the past issue aloud it highlights the label over the birthright and consequently the negative habit is reinforced.

Up until age five, there was really no definitive difference between the two; we were just acquiring and understanding information at the same time. This can be contributed to the reality that our minds are much more malleable and still being formed when we are young. We have freedom of thought and mentally similar to clay being molded –formulating the foundation of our own thoughts. Of course, with much help from the people and circumstances surrounding us. We constantly thirst for more knowledge, more information, and more know-how. It takes very little effort to search and find the information that we need (or don't need), so we tend not to process and hold information beyond the surface level of our mental capacity.

For example, when I was a young kid, before we had technology, my mind was like a steel trap. I remembered everything! So much so, my buddies would tell me the phone numbers that they wanted to remember because I never forgot anything. It's amazing to me how the capacity of my own mind was so much different then. Even when I was not thinking for myself the ability to own and understand my thoughts and abilities was much more evident than it is now. I took ownership of my impeccable memory and it became a point of reference for others to remember me by. I understood the power of this skill and owned the benefit of exercising it. So, how does one move out of the labels and into ownership with understanding? Anything worth having is worth working for, I am a witness that in addition to internal love we must take every though captive. Just as the bible instructs, it is important to meditate and read to achieve and maintain ownership of the mind.

The 95 percent thought capacity of the subconscious mind is an internal love; it is a place of submitted humility where we can just BE great without having to produce or bring forth anything. Internal love is one of the first key components I will mention as we tackle ownership of self. One cannot truly begin the process of ownership or understanding without a firm foundation of internal love. One of the most common errors in our understanding of ourselves and love is the way we are re-wired and trained by society. We began to believe that we must DO something to BECOME great or worth loving. This belief is in direct opposition to the plan of God in our lives. As his children we don't have to do much. He created us to live and walk in his love and our inherent greatness as he extends his grace to cover us in every season. His grace is indeed sufficient. However, we are bombarded with achievement-based greatness and standard-based grace, which distracts us from the loving

And now these three remain; faith, hope and love. But the greatest of these is love.
1 Corinthians 13:13

reminders that God has placed in each day. When we do not practice internal love it becomes harder for us to accept our greatness. When we do not accept our greatness we are less likely to understand and walk in our purpose. The importance of love is highlighted in 1 Corinthians 13:13.

When moving from internal love into action steps for mind mastery, its often critical to bring yourself and every thought into captivity. *Bring every thought captive in the knowledge and the obedience of Christ. (2 Cor. 10:5)* What is that –that is called faith. We can get back to really connecting with what we were given – which is our greatness –by thinking for ourselves. One of the first things I suggest that people do to begin to master their mind in this way, bringing their whole conceptual thought process under subjection, is to take time to be still. Prayer is acknowledging and thanking God for the greatness he has given and making the best effort every day to live to the fullest. God, my heavenly father, provides all that I need and it is my responsibility to participate in the natural and allow it to be expressed through me.

In Psalm 1:2, we are instructed to meditate on his words day and night. Some may label it as mediation however, for me it is prayer. Meditative prayer brings us back to a place where our thoughts are very directed because we have brought them under submission and this allows us to engage in thinking for ourselves. In the act of prayer, we are talking and having dialogue with the Creator of greatness. He is the one that doesn't makes mistakes, the one that knows all –including all of our thoughts. The enemy does not know your thoughts. He walks around like a roaring lion, seeking whom he may devour, but he is not in every place at the same time. God is! So, sit still and let God speak to you and bring you back to the mental self-control that you need to begin mastering your mindset.

In order for you to grow, you must read and make an effort to grow yourself intellectually every day. Soak up knowledge and seek understanding of what it is you are learning. If you want to reprogram yourself, you have to fight the counterproductive programming that is already seeped its way into your subconscious. We have television programs that we set schedules around and set our DVRs to grab entertainment when cannot clear the calendar. These things literally take us away from faith because they brings us into mindset of what is not real. After which, we have a hard time differentiating from reality and falseness. It is amazingly sad how we will do that but we won't read. It is what separates us from our greatness.

From a metacognition standpoint these things are all critical. And, if we wish to further master the mindset we have to learn to let things go. Anxiety and stress become counterproductive to mastering the mindset because, when those things are there, it is even harder for you to control the way that you think. I wrote about this in my first book, *Do*

Positive just Because: The Key to Living a Life You Have Always Imagined. All five keys in that book speak to a new existence, a new daily practice and a new daily habit that if practiced and mastered will become your default. Mastering the mind is about separating it and getting rid of all the confusion and the clutter. You will be able to distinguish the truth from noise.

The only way we are going to truly get back maintaining greatness is by reprogramming the mind to accept our rightful place. Without it one cannot uncover the greatness to explore the opportunities to build or maintain. Because mind mastery is an ongoing process it is important for one to not only understand but to engage in cultivating an atmosphere for greatness. We do this through accountability just as Romans 12:2 commands:

> *And do not be conformed to this world, but be transformed by the renewing of your mind, so that you may prove what the will of God is , that which is good and acceptable and perfect.*

2

ACCOUNTABILITY

ACCOUNTABILITY

One of the biggest misconceptions of accountability is the belief that one must answer to someone outside of themselves. While accountability does include the minor assistance of others, it ultimately puts you in the driver's seat of your life. As an athlete I understood the basics of accountability but it wasn't until I became homeless that I began to practice it. Homelessness pushed me into a place of accountability by requiring me to answer to myself FIRST. Before I could ask anyone else to hold me accountable to my goals I had to self impost the same upon myself. During the journey I became the first partner to my personal success through accountability. Personal accountability is your awareness, understanding and ownership of everything in your life.

The societal prescription for success often involves partnerships with others and reliance on limiting systems. An identifying feature of the society is little to no reliance on God. The adverse influence of regular compliance with this practice becomes a pattern involving lack of personal accountability, which is also known as "learned helplessness." Learned helplessness enables the false idea that you are not enough and therefore are incapable of planning, starting, and executing goals related to your greatness. Dismissal of the active compliance with the societal remedy is initiated by activation of personal ownership. When operating outside of ownership of self we are unaware of our greater gifts. In my first book, *Do Positive Just Because: The Keys to Living the Life You Always Imagined*, the first key is "Own It." Ownership of self is a critical piece to maintaining greatness because the societal norm clearly leads to dependency.

Personal accountability often ends the patterns of allowing others to think for us while enabling a reflective view of our lives. As I ended a phase of frustration during the season of homelessness, I had to first own where I was and identify where I was trying to go. When one becomes the driver of their own life, he/she must first identify the route to take in order to reach the desired destination. Directional questions are vital to accountability because they require us create contracts with our inner greatness. I was taught

> *Therefore, if anyone is in Christ, he is a new creature; the old things passed away; behold new things have come."*
> *2Corinthians 5:17*

that education and traditional employment were necessary steps to obtaining "The American Dream." My life required me to dismiss this belief once I became new in Christ and focused on activation of the greater gifts.

The average person has over 6,000 thoughts a day, and over ninety percent of those thoughts are negative. This is why accountability must become a primary practice. When we activate the position of personal accountability, we commit to the private responsibility of owning our thoughts –both positive and negative. When you own your thoughts you are actively thinking for yourself and taking every thought captive to inspect it further. Allowing others to think for us and then placing blame on them for our mistakes has become a subconscious habit –one we do constantly without even noticing it. We do it on autopilot and often unintentionally become the passenger as someone else drives our car. Eventually we're upset that we are not where we want to be but we avoid the reality that we relinquished control and released it to someone else. Personal accountability forces us to continuously dig deeper in order to evaluate our direction and progress. A lot of our individual outcomes are a result of individual upbringing and exposure. Early programming sets the foundation of the psyche. If we are taught the benefits of accountability at a young age, then we are more likely to develop the practice and appreciation for it. However, if one is not introduced to the personal responsibility they are more likely to become passengers and therefore prisoners to life.

In order to begin the process of personal accountability, we must be aware of our thought patterns. Change comes from an intentional awareness of programming. I knew exactly how I became homeless once I was able to identify the errors in my thinking. Once I knew the actions and thoughts that led to my displacement, I relied on God's word to create new thoughts.

We are commanded in Philippians 4 to dwell on the true, honorable, right, good and lovely thoughts. The passage further challenges us to fix our focus on things worthy of praise while guarding out hearts and minds in Christ Jesus. Throughout the maintenance process I reinforce this command because repetition is a key component to developing accountability in the mind. We must truly grasp the power of the subconscious mind over the conscious one. This is the essence of meta-cognition and making the shift to consciously be accountable for all of our thoughts.

Let's evaluate accountability and greatness as it relates to employment. Most of us don't have positions of creativity or innovation where we work. The majority of employees have positions with unexciting activities that they probably do not enjoy. The same actions are repeated, work becomes predictable and comfortable so they don't have to really think about much to be "productive." Many people know what their job entails, how long it takes and the depth of each assignment. Thus, they don't bother to go beyond the limits and they accept jobs that can be done within the eight hour time frame just to make ends meet. Once the unfulfilling occupation is finished the rest of the day is filled with social media, personal pleasures, parenting tasks or ongoing thoughts of meeting a work quota. Each year, their professional evaluation shows that they meet the requirements and sufficiency standards, they receive a livable wage, and things remain that way for as long as they are willing to follow that cycle. Individuals who choose this path may achieve daily success but never really experience the greater joy of excelling. If at some point they choose their greatness, the thought patterns of their daily life will change. Instead of being satisfied with that ordinary their mind, almost instantaneously, becomes consumed with breaking out of the mundane. Thoughts of thriving become the daily driving force, they create new goals and hold themselves accountable.

In order to be fully accountable, it is required that we take care of ourselves in every area -spiritually, mentally, emotionally, and PHYSICALLY. Our bodies are the temple of God, yet most of us do not take the best care of them. We consciously and continually relinquish that responsibility, eventually becoming lazy and slothful. Then it comes to physical health, we only seem to make an effort

Or do you know that your body is a temple of the Holy Spirit who is in you, whom you have from God, and that you are not your own?
1 Corinthians 6:19

when a deficiency is brought to our attention. When something feels wrong or pains us, we tend to rely on the wisdom of a medical professional without regard to our own misuse of our temple. We must be accountable for our well being before the diagnosis, prognosis, or threat. We must own our health and engage in preventative measures. Society makes our lack of accountability for our health very convenient, and we must risk inconvenience to successfully undo all the thinking that got us to this place. We must think for ourselves!

Our thinking has been shifted and directed in a way that is conducive for someone else's benefit. For instance, how many times can you recall rushing through a fast food line to grab an unhealthy lunch or dinner instead of making healthy choices or planning ahead? One of the most poisonous things we consume on a daily basis isn't cocaine or crack, IT'S SUGAR! Our God-given temples are being destroyed by our lack of accountability with regard to health and nutrition. It takes intentionality to destroy unhealthy habits and eliminate excuses. We must hold ourselves accountable for what we allow into our temples because what we feel and how we think can be directly linked to our eating habits.

This may be one of the hardest areas to develop and maintain accountability because it requires more intent and planning. As difficult as it may be, we must force ourselves to make changes to create physical health. I have found that the discipline developed through actively working towards physical health assists with building discipline and accountability in other areas of life. For instance, a morning routine of walking creates a habit of waking earlier, eating a balanced breakfast and may actually reduce tardiness. Physical accountability is critical to move forward in life free of preventable illness and disease.

Once we reach a place of personal, physical and occupational accountability we may find it easier to navigate in relationships also. This is the most common type of accountability practiced. Relationship accountability governs how we act and react within all of our relationships. We have to be accountable for the nature of these relationships, how they are formed, and how intentional we are about their development. I'm not saying all of this is easy, but ultimately understanding the importance and responsibility you have is paramount to succeeding in your own life. Emotional accountability, once we understand that our feelings are merely representations and mirror images of our thoughts, begins to enhance maturity and definitely fosters better relationships. It all flows harmoniously together as a one begins to apply the practices and principles that lead to greatness.

Furthermore, the greatest responsibility that we have is our accountability to the original plan of the Creator. He knew upfront that we couldn't do it perfectly, which is why he sent Jesus. He knew that we would need an advocate, so he extended grace through sending His son, so we would not have to live under the law. Jesus said himself in John 10:10, "...but I come that [you] may have life, life to its fullest measure!" Unfortunately, being accountable to God has always been taught to us from a legalistic perspective. Legality leads to a relationship with God that is fear based; He (God) is not

"...but I come that [you] may have life, life to its fullest measure!" John 10:10

feared based. There is nothing but faith when it comes to God. We must understand and be accountable to His ways, forever acknowledging them in our lives.

When we do these things, our level of accountability has to grow in every area of our life: financially as stewards over all He has given; relationally because He created us for community; physically because we are his workmanship; mentally because our minds are renewed and transformed through his word. The list could go on for ages. There are so many areas that we need to be accountable in our lives. It is a significant representation of maintaining greatness to apply these principles. The basis of accountability says, "I have messed up, and I can start over." The truth of accountability says, "I see where I've fallen short, but I can pick up the pieces and begin again from here." The strength of accountability says, "I'm thinking on my own, and I am going to create the abundant life that God intended for me." Find one area in which you can become more accountable today and take steps toward your greatness.

LUKE 12:48
…Great gifts mean great responsibilities; greater gifts, greater responsibilities! (Msg.)

INTENTIONAL LIVING
CONFESSION & ACTION

Philippians 3:12-14 (NASB)
Not that I have already obtained it or have already become perfect, but I
press on so that I may lay hold of that for which also I was laid hold of by
Christ Jesus. Brethren, I do not regard myself as having laid hold of it yet; but
one thing I do: forgetting what lies behind and reaching or what lies ahead I
press on toward the goal for the prize of the upward call of God in Christ Jesus.

INTENTIONAL LIVING

When we live intentionally, we act not only ON purpose but also FOR a purpose. This has everything to with clear direction. When we can see clearly, we can create more than our minds could have ever imagined. I remember trying out for sports. I was extremely intentional in my actions to avoid being cut from the team. My actions married my pursuit and, as a result, I was always chosen because of the a stellar athlete I created. If we are going to maintain greatness, we have to be intentional about what we create. In the previous chapter on accountability, we discussed the detrimental results of conformity and systematic living. I must make it clear – systematic, thoughtless living is not intentional living.

Understand that we are the workmanship of a Creator who was beyond purposeful. Once we grasp the realization that we were made in His image, we can also do as he does –create. God spoke everything into existence. He knew exactly what He purposed; He was very intentional about every aspect of His creation down to the very order in which He created it.

CONFESSSION

There is something transformational about acknowledging an issue and intentionally choosing to overcome it. Confession allows an individual to create an outcome that cannot be manipulated by others. This is often one of the hardest acts because it requires transparency. If we want to overcome an obstacle, the acknowledgment of the issue brings us to a point of change. Often times confession allows motives and agendas to become easily identifiable. When I became conscious of my sex addiction, I was in denial until I acknowledged the problem. The declaration of guilt opened the door to intention because I no longer wanted to be chained to my compulsions. The awareness that something needed to change caused a shift in my actions. After the confession, I imposed my power over the addiction. One of the many results of intentional living is the ability to apply our authority to every situation and circumstance. Two people that serve as excellent illustrations for this are Michael Jordan and Mohammed Ali. These great men were each able to use their gifting to reinforce their willpower and take charge.

If we confess our sins, he is faithful and just to forgive us of our sins and cleanse us from all unrighteousness.
1 John 1:9

Michael Jordan imposed his strength of character on every single person he encountered when it came to basketball; he went to another level. Mohammed Ali proclaimed himself to be the greatest before he even proved it in the ring; he was in a different mental space –set apart –and he imposed his spirit. Both of these legends were intentional about both their actions and their words.

We tend to marvel at the people who overcome obstacles like poverty and, in the end, realize their greatness and experience boundless success. Those rags to riches stories belong to some of world's most successful people. The fact is, most of them came from nothing and became something because they were intentional about it. Despite labels, restrictions, lack, and all other forms of opposition, they knew what they were after and made a commitment to continue to rise above circumstances to truly be great. This does not make them better than you or me, but it did make them aware that the greatness on the inside of them could flourish beyond what they could imagine. They confessed their greatness before, during and after any action of maintenance.

ACTION

There's an old saying, "The road to hell is paved with good intentions." What the anonymous author of that quote should have said was, "it's paved with action-less intentions." Most of the components in our life contribute to our mental fatigue, making us less likely to act how and when we should. While the righteous intention

Say to the righteous that it will go well with them, For they will eat the fruit of their actions.
Isaiah 3:10

may rest in our mind, the action is carried out by a different will. Isaiah chapter 3 gives a clear outcome for righteous living in verse 10. Thus, part of intentional living is action. Just like faith without works is dead, intent without action is fruitless. Clarity in thought, direction, and purpose is intentional, but most of us don't even know what we're supposed to be doing. When intentional action steps are missing, so we tend to accept the misleading notion that if we look like everyone else everything is fine. Once you acknowledge your thread of greatness you become different and set apart in a good way. That doesn't mean everything is perfectly wrapped and protected from life's challenges, but that, at the very least, people should be able to look at us as a model of intentional action and abundant living.

One of my hardest obstacles to overcoming addition was being intentional about the things I did not do. It was easy to pair action with good intent because I knew how to act on what was right. Once I confessed my shortcoming the focus shifted to healthy and intentional avoidance. Certain actions were no longer acceptable because I held myself accountable for my actions. God entwined the thread of greatness in our lives before they even began. Somewhere along the way we have decided that greatness as achievable but only in certain areas; we often don't think total greatness is achievable. Greatness is not something that only athletes, entertainers, pastors, doctors, lawyers and entrepreneurs get to achieve. They are easily identifiable because they are highly intentional in reaching their success. They engage in healthy avoidance by only associating themselves with people, places and things that will assist in the development their greatness. Some people think that if they are not esteemed highly then greatness is off the table, but greatness at any table where your passion is served.

Intentional living means choosing to carry out actions that allow maximization of opportunities to serve, beyond the assignment and on purpose. When you make it a point to intentionally serve, God's grace will always be sufficient. We were mandated to live an abundant life of intentionality. That means every decision –from who we date, to where we go, and how we show up in the world –must be purposeful. When we engage in healthy avoidance we are able to nurture our greatness and surround ourselves with others who embody life, the way God intended it. John the Baptist wrote that he, above all things, wanted them (his followers) to prosper just as their souls prospered. Your soul prospering is a definite by-product of greatness. Consequently, when we choose not to live intentionally in all areas of our lives, we struggle more than we normally ought to.

The Bible said Job was a man who feared God and was intentional about living for the Lord. Everything he did he was recognized as intentional. He was such a model of intentional living that the enemy asked and was granted permission to go after him –his relationships, his health, and his livelihood. Job lost it all, but because he knew who he was, he never accused God. Instead Job revealed, "The one thing that feared has come upon me." Inside of Job there was fear, just like in most of us. So, the one thing that he feared came upon him. Losing all his stuff, losing what was close to him –that was his fear. The enemy attacks in areas that we're not full, in areas where we live in fear. But God knew where his heart really was. The grace of God has was sufficient for Job, and we all know that Job had twice as much in the end as he did in the beginning. If you are committed to the intent, the condition of your heart is toward the right thing.

Intentional living is an applicable key to maintaining greatness. In what area(s) of your life do you need to get more intentional? Where do you need to put more focus? You have to, right now and intentionally, make a change! Challenge yourself to stop repeating the actions of your past and open your mind to the possibilities of your greatness.

At this point we have reviewed three necessary concepts for maintaining your greatness. I challenge you to work on them before continuing to the next chapters . Develop awareness and understanding and intentionally apply it to your life. You have to get up early if you don't get up early; read if you don't already read; exercise if you don't exercise and eat better if you don't already eat well. Start today by simply meditating on the word, intentionally. When you are faced with a challenge, if someone else has already faced and beaten that challenge, then we have no excuse. If one person has been healed from cancer, then somebody else can be healed from cancer; if one person can go from being homeless to successful, so can we. If an unhappy person can go from overweight to healthy; go through three failed marriages and then finally get it right; go through financial devastation and come back to live an amazing life, so can you. If someone can go through the loss of family members; devastating destruction to their body and belongings and still find the courage to get up in the morning, smile and get it all back just like Job, SO CAN YOU! The work of healthy avoidance and intentional action contribute to one of my greatest triumphs over addiction. Intentional living may be challenging but it is not impossible, we must run to win as commanded in 1 Corinthians 9:24-27:

1 Corinthians 9:24-27
24 Do you know not know that those who run in a race all run, but only one receives the prize? Run in such a way that you may win. 25 Everyone who competes in the games exercise self- control in all things. They then do it to receive a perishable wreath, but we an imperishable.26 therefore I run in such a w, as not beating the air;27 but I discipline my body and make it my slave, so that, after I have preached to others, I myself will not be disqualified.

NUTURING RELATIONSHIPS

"If you want to go quickly, go alone. If you want to go farther, go together."

NURTURING RELATIONSHIPS

After mastering the mindset, establishing meaningful associations, and engaging with our intention, nurturing relationships is a practice that allows us to maintain greatness with longevity. Greatness involves others but, unfortunately, there here is no blueprint for relationships. In my sports career as a coach, I developed a clear understanding of the power of nurturing relationships. I discovered the benefit of nurturing relationships as many young men entered my life through the common thread of sports. Each player exhibited a unique skill set, and, as the coach, it was my responsibility to assist along the journey of uncovering and maximizing their gifts. Nurturing requires an understanding of your position within the relationship. We must understand who we are within a relationship to engage in the nurturing process. When we nurture a relationship, we empower greatness. Empowerment gives greatness permission to take root, while nurturing feeds the seed.

We see an example of God's design for relationship in the very beginning when he established intimacy with Adam

"It is not good for man to be alone, I will make him a helper suitable to him."
Genesis 2:18

and Eve. It's evident that relationships are valuable to the Creator, so how much more valuable should they be to us. By nurturing the connections we have with others, we experience the generous, abundant greatness that can only happen within the confines of relationship. I focus on adult relationships on the path to maintaining greatness because, we choose this type of relationship for ourselves-through association. It is critical that we establish healthy ways to cultivate these connections because they allow us to reach our highest potential.

Every young man I encountered as a coach shared a universal dream of becoming a professional athlete. They craved a platform where their talents were prized with financial gain and adoration. The players who were nurtured seemed to go further than those who were not. The select few, who were not in nurturing relationships outside of the team, constantly sought out opportunities to shine as individuals instead of as team members. As the coach, my role was to highlight the power of the team. Instilling the since of community was the first step to success for the athletes both personally and professionally. Many of the young men went on to become great fathers, husbands and professionals, and some still attribute their ability to navigate relationships to the lessons learned in the nurturing process. Greatness is all about other people; it's all about relationship. No one can be great by himself/herself! No matter what iconic plateau or apex they get to, there is always someone else helping. There were other people that played a part in the overall success or the recognition of the greatness.

INTENTIONAL RELATIONSHIPS

For most children, it's their parents; a musician has a band; a great player has a team; a NASCAR driver his the pit crew; a golfer a cabby; and a husband, his wife. There's always someone else involved in our success. It is our individual responsibility to attach intent to our nurturing of these relationships if the ultimate desire is greatness. So whether it's a coworker, a workout partner, or a romantic relationship, we must discover what connections we share, be intentional about collaboration, and create together for the good of everyone else around us.

Intentional praise of a partner in the relationship pulls up weeds of frustration and plants seeds of growth. When I receive calls from a former player on any team I coached, it not only nurtures the relationship but it confirms the growth of a seed. The consistent praise allows me to maintain my greatness while continuing my role as a coach for others. One of my most favorite stories to share involves possibly the best player I have ever encountered-Gerald Jerome Kohn. He struggled, more than rest of the team, with my with decision to implement early morning practices. This level of discipline was so different for the players because it required a new level of commitment, a level that, unbeknownst to them, could be carried into their personal and professional lives. The early morning practices planted the seed of timeliness and submission to authority. Years later, Gerald was intentional in his efforts to provide praise for the seed that the early morning practice provided. He is able to easily rise early and organize his day because he nurtured the intentional seed of timeliness in his youth. For some of the players my tough love was the closet to a father that they had ever had. I made it my business to praise them for their growth and encourage improvements. Once I planted the seed, the maintenance became their job and in most cases I witnessed the fruit of our labor as it flourished and they began planting new seeds into others.

NURTURING THE "WHY"

Most of us make the choice to create a relationships through points of connection alone. We find something that we like or have in common, and develop the relationship from there. Very rarely do we start the connection by considering the reasons why. We must move beyond simply liking a person and enjoying their company to intentionally defining a reason –a why. For example, you connect with a person because you both like collecting silver pens. What happens if one of you stops liking silver pens at some point? Or what if you stopped liking basketball or drag racing, or gardening. Now, you've eliminated the point of connection that had a prominent place of importance in the relationship. In other words, you have literally created a conditional relationship based merely on a shared interest. The vast majority of our interactions and bonds are formed in shallow dry ground and cannot grow to their fullest potential because of this reason. They are based on how we feel, what we share, and other one-sided aspects of our identity. This type of relationship does not maintain greatness because it does not require greatness. Participants within this type of relationship never truly grasp an understanding of the true essence of relationship –the fullness of agape (unconditional) love. Once we clearly define the reason for choosing to connect, we unlock the door to a full relationship where changes do not shift the love.

While shallow connection may have an undeniable a role in the relationship, it is more important to have a clear understanding of the why before digging deeper into collaboration and creation. The intimate extensions of who you are nurture that relationship. Pause to take inventory of your relationships and ask: Am I open and available for this person? Am I helping this person to become all that they can be? Is this person making sure that I become all I can be? These answers become the essence of beginning to nurture relationships. Ultimately, the relationship should be about being able to achieve greatness together. If you start asking questions each day like: What I can create with my partner today? How can we collaborate to make the world a better place? What can I do with my partner today to create more ease in our lives? How can we both focus on the same goal? It's not a condition of us just being together for the sake of it, but looking at the bigger picture of what we can do for the greater good. It's the same thing with our children. If we get to play and create together, instead of always telling them what to do, we empower them to walk in their greatness and strengthen the relationship at the same time. The essence of creation is an integral part of who we are as we were made like our Creator.

PRACTICAL STEPS FOR NURTURING RELATIONSHIPS

The active engagement in the process of nurturing requires us to be kind, consistent and truthful in communication. Dr. Barton Goldsmith, a renowned psychotherapist, suggests that those same three requirements are simple daily practices that can help us to nurture relationships effectively if we are intentional in our efforts. We live in a society crippled by technology and fueled by passive aggressive communication. There is a difference in our communication style when we are doing most of our interacting through social media and text messaging. The communication isn't always honest, it is often inconsistent, and we can hide behind the mystery. So, it's very hard for people to be honest and we don't open up. Kindness is a byproduct of nurturing relationships and honesty is the ultimate reward for consistency. When we are consistently kind we build a rapport within any relationship. Once we have build credibility, partners are able to truly nurture in healthy ways.

Once we have created an atmosphere of kindness, consistency and truth we must be willing to do the work to maintain it. Both parties must convey a willingness to work through difficulties and disagreements. When the why is clear, it becomes easier for individuals to face the discomforts and challenges that come with differing opinions and ideologies. As a father, husband, business owner and friend I've had my fair share of personal challenges. Total commitment to my greatness has enabled me to really walk into a place of personal growth. I had to nurture relationships that assisted in the development. The maintenance process of greatness is about working through difficulties. The resolution of the difficulty may not repair the relationship, but the act of working through the difficulty is all about your personal growth and you becoming better. It's all about you being who you need to be. I found that a better ME always leads to better "we".

Another related practice is being able to admit mistakes and to talk about them. Truth be told, we all screw up. Learning to understand the mistakes that you or your partner make will turn your life around and give you more time for joy. This all goes back to owning where you are today. You have to know who you are and know that you, like all others, sometimes fall short. But you have to learn to let go of those mistakes and allow others to own their mistakes too. Even though they may occur, and maybe even repeat, grace and love will allow for less frequent and less impacting. Partners find peace in knowing that there's a place they can go to find themselves, be themselves and still experience unconditional love.

Another thing you have to do according to Dr. Goldsmith is have a sense of humor! God has some fun. And a bit of a distraction from the rigors of daily life is essential, if we're going to have time to nurture relationships. You must commit to nurturing a life that is exciting and fun. You have to laugh. Laughing and having fun creates positive thoughts and feelings, which lead to positive attitudes and actions. Get a hobby —a welcomed

> *"Laughter doeth good like a medicine."*
> Proverbs 17:22

distraction that is going to take you into that place of feeling good and appreciating who you are. It's unbelievably attractive to have a sense of humor, to be able to laugh at yourself and laugh at others. For me, my distraction is golf. It's a fun thing to do, and my passion, my love, my desire. It provides a truly amazing feeling for me. I've incorporated that into my life and it makes me laugh and encourages me to create different connections with really good people that have the same passion. The energy is high frequency and the vibration continues to rise when we are together in that environment.

NURTURING ROMANTIC RELATIONSHIPS

Sharing life lessons and also sharing intimacy, romance and

sex are two more practices that lead to a well-nurtured relationship with your partner. When you discover something about life or yourself, and you make self-correcting moves that are healthy for your relationship with your partner, you will be surprised at the positive response you receive. This is critical; sharing life lessons only happens tentatively for some people. They only share when it is safe. But there are times when we have to express or share a lesson without the guarantee that it will be accepted, understood or applauded. In these instances, it is important to share anyway. Maybe in the past something didn't turn out right, or maybe your partner, husband or wife judged your behavior or expressed resentment regarding past failures. That possibility is sometimes present, but we have to feel good about communicating whether they embrace it, accept it, believe it or not! Of course, it is a hallmark of a healthy relationship to be on one accord and to be advocates for one another, but it's still something that you have to practice. You have to be able to discuss life lessons, the things you read, the concepts you meditate on, the ideas you dream of, and the things that God downloads onto your hard drive. In addition, love, intimacy, romance and sex are the cornerstones of a loving relationship. Being good roommates just won't cut it. There has to be the desire to be together as a couple. You may think the spark is gone but there are too many ways to rekindle it. All you have to do is try.

This chapter is all about relationships, but truly maintaining greatness is about the marriage relationship. It truly is about re-establishing that and moving closer to marriage as a integral part of the foundation of society as a whole. Today it is being attacked and torn down and it doesn't have the same value respect that it used to. But it has to be respected. I've even been guilty of not respecting it the way that I should. Not giving all it required of me was something I had to shift in my life, and making that change has allowed my marriage to flourish.

Dr. Goldsmith explains that emotional support, validation and compliments play a major role in relationships. If you don't feel that your partner likes and respects you, then the connection will be weakened. You have to lift each other up. They need to be your biggest fan you need to be their biggest fan. Affirmation is a positive thing especially for people you care about. We talk about affirming our kids all the time – speaking positive, life-giving words into their live and letting them know that they are worthy, successful, great. This builds an emotional rapport with them. They feel validated and supported. So you have to have this emotional support and validation. What we do for our children, God also does for us. Because of your lineage, your DNA, God extends His grace to you, lifting you up and validating your greatness.

A major part of this is sharing goals and dreams also. We are happier when we are working toward a goal together. So, make sure you always have something to look forward to and that you are pursuing it as a couple. Again, I'm really talking about the couple connection in nurturing relationships. I think often times when one person is a dreamer and one person is not, it's very hard. Similarly, when the one person is fearful, it can be problematic if the other person is faithful. When one partner is doubtful and the other is confident, there is always a push and pull –a tug of war that doesn't allow you to move, as a unit, in the dream space together. But if you all want to go together with a new habit of nurturing the relationships, you must have dreams and goals that resonate with both of you.

In the Old Testament, Amos asked, "How can two walk together, lest they agree?" Often times we will allocate our dreams to somebody else and just line up with their desires, even though we don't genuinely want to and vice versa. That inauthentic energy is felt by the other person and can lead to resentment, misunderstanding, and the death of dreams. Couples who share dreams and new experiences together develop a stronger bond. They do things together that take them out of normalcy, out of their comfort zone, add spontaneity and establish a new level of trust. There has to be an enthusiastic desire to live, grow, and achieve on that next level.

Lastly, major keys to nurturing relationships are compassion, acceptance and forgiveness. If you are together for a while there will be lots of challenges, and possibly some things you just can't fix. But knowing that you have that person to work through difficult things together with, creates a lasting bond that is not easily broken. If you understand this, you'll understand true greatness, as it is in service but also in forgiveness. Forgiveness is where grace is, and that is of the utmost importance in relationships. Compassion, acceptance and forgiveness are all representations of nurturing unconditional love.

Nurturing relationships is a way to restore and maintain great male-female, husband-wife relationships. In the end, it's not only a way to greatness, and it is necessary to maintain. Now again, all of this is predicated on you. Begin by mastering the mindset and understand that these relationships are part of positive association. Nurturing is an intentional way to connect, collaborate and create. All of those things have to be there in order for the relationships to be nurtured.

Two are better than one, because they have a good reward for their toil. For if they fall, one will left up his fellow. But woe to hi who is alone when he falls and has not another to lift him up! Again, if two lie together, they keep warm, but how can one keep warm alone? And though a man might prevail against one who is alone two will withstand him — a threefold cord is not quickly broken.

Ecclesiastes 4:9-12

THANKFULNESS
OPPORTUNITY & RESPONSIBLITY

All things work together for good for them that love God and those who are called according to his purpose.

Romans 8:28

THANKFULNESS

Thankfulness creates the opportunity to think on the good things in life. The Bible instructs us to give thanks in all things, good, bad, or indifferent. Gratitude is the next level expression of the command to be thankful. When we are able to position ourselves within this command, we graduate to active expressions and next level actions. Eventually, we can effortlessly weave it into our greatness and maintenance process. The expression of gratefulness is the answer to how you actively feel and engage with anyone you encounter. It is a reminder of the goodness of God, the unconditional love that he lavishes on us, especially when it comes to the area of grace. This is

Give thanks to the Lord, for he is good; his love endures forever
1 Chronicicles 16:34

one of the areas that we should practice zealous thankfulness. When we consider all that we have been afforded, we are really indebted to God for grace. We should indeed be thankful for another chance. We must be thankful for life and all the things that come with our daily existence. Thankfulness is merely a gesture, an acknowledgement that we recognize God's grace and mercy daily. Thankfulness creates the constant opportunity to shift out thoughts from problems to praise.

OPPORTUNITY

Greatness cannot be maintained without gratitude.

One must be able to look beyond the struggles and focus on the good in any situation. This creates an opportunity of growth and self-evaluation. We must be thankful for everything we have, all the opportunities we have been afforded, and we must live from the perspective of opportunity versus obligation. Obligation says, "I have to" or "It is my responsibility" But opportunity says, "I get to" and "It is my privilege." Both the positive and not so positive aspects of our lives provide opportunities for growth and development, taking us closer to realizing, actualizing, and exercising the greatness within. We are children of the Most High God, and His power (according to The Word) provides us with "everything we need pertaining to life and godliness." When someone does something for us, we make the effort or gesture of being thankful. We respond in the affirmative when we say thank you. Thankfulness is an expression. It is shown by acknowledging someone else's effort towards doing something for us or acknowledging that something beneficial and valuable was added to our lives. What I mean is, thankfulness is a natural response to a gift. Each day we rise and inhale, we experience a gift. When we do not recognize the gift, we rob ourselves of the opportunity to be thankful.

RESPONSIBLITY

There will always be opportunities for us to be thankful along the path to maintaining greatness. It is our responsibility to seize the opportunity and create a everlasting "attitude of gratitude." Once I activated the attitude of gratitude within my blended family, the process became easier. Thankfulness is the first responsibility, but greatness lies in the expression of gratitude. My oldest daughter came to me recently to share a very personal experience in her life. Immediately I became overwhelmed with thankfulness for the opportunity to assume the role of father in her life when I married her mother. I intentionally paused before speaking during our dialogue allowing gratitude to be expressed through the words of wisdom I shared. My words of appreciation empowered her to choose her own path without wrestling with the idea of hurting me. This experience comes to mind because it helps me to understand how gratitude takes thankfulness to another level.

We must stand firm in thankfulness, by first acknowledging what we have been given, and then seal it with a constant application of gratitude. Most parents teach their toddler to say "thank you" even though they may not really understand the depth of sacrifice made for them. Once a toddler moves into adolescent years, he begin to develop the ability to understand sacrifice and rewards. This understanding enables him to maintain behaviors that result in rewards and avoid the ones connected to unpleasant penalties. Once the adolescent grows in age and maturity, he takes his actions to the next level and truly begins to understand the "thank you" learned as an infant.

Gratitude is more than just a learned behavior, it's a state of existence; it is a conscious expression of acknowledgment and maturity. Maintaining greatness is about being responsible enough to take thankfulness to the next level. If someone does something that makes you feel good, you acknowledge what they did and respond with an act of gratitude of your own. When things are positive in life we experience moments of total peace and happiness. Maintenance of the feelings is a personal responsibility guided by reflections of gratitude and actions of thankfulness. When you walk in the application of gratitude you tend to attract more things and people on your level. The daily habit of being thankful, not only for the good but also for things that aren't what you would like, that should be the attitude. It's a mindset; It's grace personified. While learning to maintain greatness, we have to remain faithfully grateful. It's an appreciative attitude towards whatever life brings, not just recognition or an announcement. It truly is how we should live.

I explain more about this in the fourth concept in my book "*Do Positive Just Because*" within a chapter focused on finding the good in everything. That's what thankfulness looks like in a practical way. A daily acceptance of what is happening in your life comes with the responsibility to accept the idea that that God uniquely planned your existence. When we take this to the next level, it becomes easier to find the good in everything. Essentially, we are acknowledging a responsibility to recognize that everything happening in our lives is purposeful. This is one of the biggest challenges for most people. Personal responsibility is a choice worth making, especially when it comes to the active practice of thankfulness.

THINK THANKFUL

At some point in life everyone must make the choice to push past frustrations from negative speech and actions. This is why I addressed subconscious programming, upbringing, and associations the previous chapters. Those are the main areas of our lives that suffocate our recognition and maintenance of greatness. The natural programming of our thoughts is to see the glass as half empty instead of half full. Seeing the glass as half full requires us to reprogram a from posture of discontentment to thankfulness. Changing our perspective to gratefulness, helps us to tap into our greatness. To be content, like Paul, who learned that the secret of true contentment is to rely on the strength that comes only from the creator living within us. This is how we create a deliberate and consentient practice of finding the good in everything —deliberate gratefulness takes thankfulness to the next level.

Maintaining greatness is about next level living. This level functions in the opportunity of thankfulness and takes hold to the responsibility of gratitude. God sent Jesus so that we could have an abundant life, a life beyond our wildest dreams. When we serve with an attitude of gratitude, that service is an expression of greatness. So, when we really begin to practice and embrace gratitude, it becomes a habit. Activation of the new habit creates an atmosphere energized by our everyday existence. We are then thankful for the past and walking in gratitude, which creates excitement for the future. Living your life in this anticipatory way makes you even more open to discovering what else you have to be grateful for –and the cycle continues. You can't wait to experience what is coming, favor and opportunity rise when gratitude is amplified. It's tremendous how finding the good in everything is a simple way to perpetually remain in your greatness.

Each day we wake up with a choice – to have a good day or a bad one. Whether you choose good or bad, there is always an opportunity to change it with thankfulness, through actions of gratitude. Thankfulness is a choice, and I have found that it is impossible to be fearful, stressed or depressed and grateful at the same time. Gratitude and thankfulness enable a shift in perspective from negative to positive, from low frequency to high energy. This shift changes our thoughts, which impacts our feelings, and makes way for a change in our actions and ultimately our lives. I have found that this personal choice affects our interactions with those closest to us. My daughter was able to stop wrestling with the situation we discussed because of the atmosphere of thankfulness and words of gratitude we shared. She no longer had to worry about how I would respond because I created an intentional environment of contentment and greatness with every action. Maintaining the greatness that resides within is predicated on our ability, not only to increase our awareness and intentionality, but also to be thankful and walk in a constant state of gratitude.

ASSOCATION QUOTIENT

It is of the Lord's mercies that we are not consumed, because his compassions fail not. They are new every morning: great is they faithfulness.
Lamentations 3:22-24

ASSOCATION QUOTIENT

The association quotient is derived from three principles learned during the early foundations of education- writing reading and arithmetic. The principles assist in early development by providing building blocks for communication. One of the first things we learn is writing, we learn to spell our name and begin the process of reading. Eventually, we move to the more complex skills such as addition and subtraction to sharpen reasoning. Once we understand basic math we graduate to complex calculations which involve the understanding of number values and equations. If we carry the basics of arithmetic into our daily life, we understand our life has value just like the numbers we learn to solve an equation. We unintentionally assign a value to every area of our life through our words and actions. If we are not careful, we end up add the wrong components, resulting in an equation that is simply not solvable. Complicated equations of life and relationships begin to add up once you understanding how your mind operates and determine the value assigned to each component within it.

Maintaining greatness and has everything to do with one thing –association. Determining the value of association is very simple mathematics. People and surroundings can either add to your life, subtract from your life, multiply your life, or divide your life. The only people that you really need in your life are ones that add and multiply. For instance, during the journey to overcoming addition, it was important to surround myself with individuals who added encouragement and multiplied my faith. I understood the value in appropriate associations and immediately ended conversations that subtracted from my progress or devalued my efforts. Most associations do not require subtraction after we take personal inventory and assign or own values. The value I assigned to my total recovery was fueled by those who could add and multiply in my life. Subtraction was not necessary at this point because I had already devalued my addiction and rendered it powerless. When I surrendered my issue totally to God he divided the old man from the new and enabled me to enter a new season. Don't misunderstand this, you can love people who subtract and divide your life and sometimes they can effectively be a part of your journey towards maintaining greatness. I caution you, though, to always be aware of the association and mindful of the math. Figuring out your association quotient must come after mastering your mind. When the mind is not mastered, you may not think for yourself and assign disproportionate value to the opinions of others. Mastering your mind assigns appropriate value to your thoughts and reduces the need to constantly consult others for approval or validity. Once you master the mind it leads to a greater level of cognitive awareness and intentional associations.

As an avid athlete, I gravitated toward athletes who shared

the same quest of attaining a college scholarship. We placed value on our dream to play on the college level. We held one another accountable, and each conversation added to the knowledge of our skills and talent. The success within the associations can be measured by the fact that we all went on to play post-high school basketball. Overall our accomplishments prove to be a solid example of addition and multiplication in the process of assigning value. In retrospect, I realized that I never hung around people who would subtract or influence my demise or detriment. Even as a young adult, I placed great value in the most important areas of my life by being selective in my associations. There is an energy that marinates your life when you are surrounded by people who share common goals. The common thread creates an energy of agreement for common good –a positive goal. As outlined in the previous chapter most of us intentionally gravitate to people with that energy. We exchange ideas and have conversations fueled by a desire to improve, and our effort is directed towards accomplishing it. The hours we spend focusing in this way literally help program the subconscious and direct our everyday activities. When the people around us support our personal passion, it adds value to the passion and stimulates our desire to continue with our equation.

ASSIGNING VALUE WITHIN ASSOCATIONS

Most people don't fully understand the value within what links environment and behavior. We mirror the associations created by values in the environment where the most time is spent. Religion and the traditional education system have proven to be two of the most influential constructs of our society. These institutions have an enormous amount of control in shaping our behaviors regarding association. Unfortunately, these are the main environments that refuse to advocate for mastering the mind and restoring our God-given ability to think and reason for ourselves. These environments are catalyst for separation in our society. In all actuality, where association is concerned, the two entities do a great deal of choosing for us. Some of their ways are silently manipulative while others are obvious and intentional. Most of the seeds are planted on a subconscious level and go unnoticed, resulting in our invaluable selection of associations. Both the education system and religious system literally modeled each other in their attempt to have you live a certain way. If or when the blueprint is nurtured, it becomes much stronger than it was intended to be. Misunderstanding this makes it hard to maintain greatness because we are seduced into a life that's full of incorrectly assigned values —a life that is average and ruled by conformity and fear. These systems create fear, causing us to be afraid of engaging individually, thinking for ourselves, or teaching others to do the same. This cycle creates more fear, and this is how we get trapped into limiting lives, never unearthing the true nature of who we are within. Let's take a deeper look into how this system works.

Most feel the need to go to a church because they want to be around people like minded individuals. They all want to do great things and please God. They inherently know that associating with people of God will ultimately help to strengthen their own faith. This is a clear picture of the Association Quotient at work. It has become obvious that religious beliefs and traditions have been blended into church philosophies over time. The Bible promotes one church in Jesus Christ, yet there are hundreds if not thousands of denominations. Each denomination may practice a different belief, based on a different interpretations of the same bible. The lines of personal opinion have become so blended with

Do not be conformed to the world but be transformed by the renewing of your mind, so that you may prove what the will of God is, that which is good and acceptable and perfect.
Romans 12:2

unbiblical values that the results now reflect unclear understandings.

The heart of all religion is to direct people toward the need for a Savior and a meaningful relationship with Christ. The goal is a fruitful life here on earth and the enjoyment of a heavenly home thereafter. Instead of appropriately assigning value to godly living, religion has become a total reflection of what the world says. The church has conformed from a place or group of people that embody renewal, restoration, growth and support, to an extension of man's attempt to control and manipulate.

Before we continue I must clarify. This is not an indictment on religious organizations. This is an attempt to lead people – God's people –back to an awareness of how to appropriately assign values within religion. The goal is growth and empowered choices in association that add to life and multiply the greatness within. When one does not know and understand the depths of their actions, it's extremely hard to do anything but repeat behaviors. A true understanding of spirituality, faith, and religion empowers multiplication of greatness instead of division and subtraction through associations.

As the school system was being developed, a curriculum, created by Alexander Inglis, was endorsed by Harvard University. This curriculum outlined six functions of the educational system. The functions clearly show a deliberate and almost surgical attack on the unity of lower and middle class. Overall, the goal of the school system was very limiting and often stifled the potential of students to keep them divided and uninformed. Associations were a by-product of this separation and intentional grouping, on the part of the elite. This cycle still functions and contributes to our subconscious selection and assignment of value within associations.

The first function is an adjusted or adaptive one. It was designed to create fixed habits with little to no reasoning involved. When you are trained into fixed habits, critical thinking and judgment are annulled. Decisions are habit-based and involve very little (if any) independent thinking. The power of greatness is rooted in the ability to think independently, and without it we assign infinite value to thoughts of others.

The second function highlights the consistent practice of conformity. As children we are taught to sit still and obey the rules. We're taught to conform, be in subjection, simply listen and then do exactly as we're told. Integrating conformity into the school system was to make us as similar as possible, with no consideration to our unique differences. We have similarities yes, but no one has the same DNA or fingerprints. We are alike in our origin but we are very much unique, especially with regard to the way that we think.

The third functions are diagnostic and directive, while the fourth is differentiating. The directive function literally encourages you to accept your "proper" social role. The separation function specifies that you are only to be trained to the extent to which your social role merits. From the beginning, our proper and social role has always been royal, priestly. We're sons and daughters of the King. But we're taught that, because of race, education, status or gender, we are less than average.

Another function Inglis imposes is called the selective function, in which he distinguishes a hierarchy based on the "favored races." The Bible even talks about "the elect." I won't going to get in too deep here, but it describes an elect group of people that will be saved and go to heaven. The world also talks about the different races, one or a few always being higher, superior or better than the others. It's as if there has always been a battle to prove who should be submissive to the other.

In his final function, Inglis introduced the propaedeutic function. In it, Inglis outlines the requirement of an elite group of caretakers. Caretakers who are assigned to watch over and control the people who have been restricted, herded, and trained for certain roles. Now let's look at the hierarchy of the world we live in. We look at a functional world that says we have owners and employees; one is higher than other. In the religious circles we have pastors and then we have the congregation, and one is viewed as higher than the other. Even though each of us are men or women, even though each of us were born in the image and likeness of God, even though we are told no one's greater than the other, we perceive the opposite is true. Within these structures there is still a very apparent and obvious differentiation in the hierarchy and subjectivity of roles. There has always been a group of people that have been set up to have authority over and lead others. Revolting against the system does not mean you forfeit having mentors and people you esteem. People can most certainly influence your life. However, what Alexander Inglis and Harvard have deliberately instituted has been a violent misuse of relationship and has taken away our ability to choose our associations intentionally.

In John Gatto's *"Dumbing Us Down"* he writes about the results of the functions that Inglis injected into the DNA of the educational system. The education system is where we get most of our knowledge; the religious system and the education system mirror each other in both intent and in result. In this work, he gives us seven things that point out all the dysfunction created in us through our involvement in the system. First, he says that the school system creates confusion, leaving us bewildered and unaware –and I would advocate that the religious system does the same. The reality is that most of us live in constant confusion. We don't have singleness of thought. We don't have a clear purpose. We don't know what to do.

Truthfully, I get so many calls from people who don't know what it is they're supposed to be doing in life. They are confused, unaware of their purpose and have no earthly idea where to turn, what to do, or how to do it. This is because of their foundational way of thinking was learned through the system. They have been led away from critical thought and individuality and trained to be perpetually confused. Luckily, they don't have to remain there! God's word clearly says in 1

Corinthians 14:33 that "[He] is not the author of confusion but of peace." Because we know what His plan is for us (to prosper and live an abundant life) we know there is a way out of this perfunctory.

Gatto goes on to point out six more behaviors learned throughout one's time in the education system and the damaging costs they have on us individually and corporately – acceptance of class affiliation, leading to indifference, emotional dependence, intellectual dependence, provisional self-esteem, and fear of constant surveillance. It is a powerful thing when we realize the affect this has had on our minds and our associations. The people around us contribute directly to the reasons why we struggle to maintain the greatness that lives within. To understand that we were strategically put into this position should ignite a fire in our bellies to unlock and unleash the hidden greatness God intended to be visible to the world. Because God is gracious, he allows us to get back to that greatness if we choose to follow Him as he leads the way.

So, when we're talking about the association of all these things, they are certainly a part of how we define who we are and who we will become. Meanwhile, the associations we have formed through the lens of these misconceived constructs continue to inform our reality. The truth remains; you can't master greatness when you have a blurred view of how to form the right association. A lot of us have associated with the wrong people for what we believe are the right reasons. Education's whole goal was to make us as alike as possible, as do most the other systems in this world. We are all different and unique. We've succumbed to this imposed likeness, which makes us associate with those like us versus those that we may really need to be around. As these imposed associations take form and solidify, we aren't aware of true association. Thus, we are unaware of our true potential. Several functions within the curriculum used by the education system roll over seamlessly into religious systems. There is supposed to be a clear difference but the results of both are jarringly similar.

There are so many subsets in our culture and they drive us because this is how we are trained. Inside of us there's a need for all these things, but God should fill this need. That's where true sufficiency comes from. The Bible calls God "El Shaddai" meaning "the all breasted and all sufficient one." He has everything that we need. But because we don't understand whose child we are, we think we are lacking something that we have to find somewhere else outside of ourselves. We think there is a place for us to go or a person for us to get in relationship with in order to find what is missing. God is everything that we need; He's everything we need because he is great. He is great and you are his child therefore, you have access to all of his greatness. We are made in His image and He lives inside of us. The association quotient is a critical piece because you have to know who your true association needs to be with. When we appropriately assign value to the associations our personal equations will include addition and multiplication.

Take action to become aware of the constructs of this society that would have you dim your light. Withdraw and dispel the workings of deliberate attempts at toning your options and indirectly choosing your associations. Surround yourself with people who are doing the same –people who will lovingly lead you back to path when you get wayward. Model greatness for everyone who chooses to associate with you. We've got to be able to live and show how great we are simply because greatness is in us. Use the association quotient, do the simple math, and make it work in your favor.

"There's no success without successors and inspiring and influencing people to pursue the things in life that they've been called to do as part of you creating a lineage of success story." - TD Jakes

INFLUENCE & INSPIRATION

INFLUENCE & INSPIRATION

No matter who you are, you will have influence over someone. Our level of influence depends on the degree to which we freely share our experiences. As a mentor, I began to fully understand influence through one of the young men I impacted by the name of Richard Lee. Along the journey, our relationship developed into that similar to a father and son. Influence creates impact, and the lasting impression of impact maintains greatness. That's how simply and completely it happens. If you are on the planet, you are not only influenced, you are an influencer. The key to maintaining greatness as an influencer is to possess a positive mindset, with integrity, while moving in the right direction. All of these are critical, foundational components of using our influence to inspire greatness. Any and everyone can access this greatness, but most don't know the level of influence they possess. Richard moved into my home from his hometown in Canada. He had big goals as an athlete and believed that I could assist him in reaching them. As a surrogate father for him I held a great responsibility to positively influence his life and assist with forward movement. Maintaining greatness as an influencer involves giving to others from the greatness within you. This means we must always be aware of our greatness and this is where the challenge lies for most. The same greatness we recognize in others lives in us and is activated when we maximize all opportunities and capabilities by influencing others. The truth is, it's hard to influence or inspire someone if you do not fully grasp who you are.

We must shift our thinking from believing that the influence of someone else in our lives is greater than our ability to positively influence others. Influence happens naturally for those who engage in personal development and growth. Richard was able to maximize the opportunities within our relationship and shift from being influenced to becoming the influencer. He seamlessly transitioned to other areas of greatness in his life and continues to influence others through his gifting. Maintaining greatness in my life has allowed me to influence and inspire people, not for personal gain, but for their growth and actualization of natural potential. When people have potential that they have a hard time tapping into, coaching is the opportunity to influence and inspire them through drawing out all those hidden components of their potential. As we grow, others can simply witness the change and be inspired.

INSPIRATION

The transition from influence to inspiration involves building a bridge through self-reflection. When we engage in self-reflection we are able to identify our greatness and allow our light to shine. Inspiration is simply simulating the actions and emotions of others through verbal or physical expression.

We have the power of expressing ourselves in a way that inspires others if we are intentional. Throughout the maintenance process, it's important to measure or monitor our expressions to inspire ourselves and others. Inspiration starts when we begin the measuring process by evaluating our influence. Setting good examples daily in every action can create an atmosphere of inspiration through our influence. When we begin with ourselves and the expressions we model, it opens the door for inspiration to enter and take root. A true model can and will have flaws because we are all human but, this realization places a responsibility of intentionality onto the influencer. As a model there will always be an audience, and every action should be guided by the fruits of the spirit. Galatians Chapter 5 Verses 22-23 outline the characteristics that contribute to inspiration.

But the fruit of the Spirit is love, joy, peace, patience, kindness, goodness, faithfulness, [23] gentleness, self-control;
Galatians 5:22-23

As an influencer I am able to operate in love with joy, patience, kindness, faithfulness and self control. For me, the evidence of this practice is clear in the previously mentioned story of Richard. I eventually had an opportunity to speak with his biological father. During our conversation he recognized the fruits of the spirit that I practiced in my daily life. Incorporating the expressions allowed my influence to plant the seed of inspiration in Richard. The seed became a strong tree with ripe fruit. I was intentional in my actions because I was aware of the audience and the power of walking in my greatness. Whether you want to believe it or not, people watch you. They watch what you do, how you react, and how you respond. There is a unique difference between one who reacts immaturely, driven by emotions and unaware of their influence, and one who reacts maturely. Individuals who maintain greatness and operate in the fruit of the spirit remain steady even through a storm. They are aware of their greatness and unafraid to measure or monitor their expressions. Evaluation for maintenance allows us to reflect on our expressions and monitor actions to inspire others to grow into their greatness.

During moments of monitoring influence and inspiration it is important evaluate the heart. An effective influencer must have a heart for people. One of the most powerful quotes was introduced to me by a influencer by the name of Vaughn McLaughlin. The quote simply says, "People don't care how much you know until they know how much you care." I've kept it in my mind, often using it as a guide. Having a heart for others challenges us to think outside of our needs and wants. Again I caution you, this is no easy task. Psalm chapter 73 verse 26 warns us of this in saying *"the flesh and heart may fail, but God is the strength of my heart and my portion forever"*. Having a heart for others inspires humility as we serve in the capacity of an influencer. Humility allows greatness to shine through and paves the way for inspiration. As a father, I have learned that humility allows me to influence my children in an impactful way. One of the challenges that caused me to check my heart was within my blended family. As the step father, I had to become ok with the idea of my oldest daughter speaking to her biological father. I examined my heart and my love for her was stronger than any negative emotion I felt or thought I had. Once I realized this, I was able to inspire her to expand her thinking and dive into the possibilities of a relationship with her father. Inspiration begins with those closest to us because they hold a special place in our heart.

Once I became confident in my position within my family, I was able uplift my children as I influenced them. One very important thing to assess is whether or not you are encouraging others or bring them down. Are you present and supportive when people are going through hard times? Are you there when they're struggling with who they are or who they want to be? Are you that person they can count on for a perfect word or a listening ear? All of these questions will reveal to you how much you actually care for others.

If you want to continue to inspire people you have to be transparent. When you are seeking to inspire others, transparency is an important characteristic because people see the glory but they don't always know the story. Most people have no idea what others go through, but glory is a direct reflection of one being tried, tested, and challenged, then overcoming all of it to present a finished product. This doesn't mean that they need to know every last bit of your information, but there are a lot of things you can put on the table that will allow them to see your humanity and transcendence.

The Bible tells a story of three men who came through fire and did not smell of smoke. Since they did not smell like the experience, others may not understand the faith that they developed during the trial. The victory was evident but the entire story was not eveident. For an influencer this can be challenging because others can get the misconception that maintaining greatness is easy. In my mind, I imagine the three men happily telling the story and inspiring others to believe in the God that delivered them. When you open yourself up and share from the heart, you give access to judgmental people, critics –those who don't want to look at themselves. I am sure the three men encountered a few doubters but, because they had a heart for people and a mission to uplift God, they continued on. The vulnerability was worth the risk because they understood their position of influence. When you become vulnerable enough to tell your story and inspire others, it is important to keep the mission in mind. Confidently sharing from a mature place allows others to be inspired to unlock their true potential. Openness creates a common ground for individuals using the thread of imperfection. It takes imperfect people to influence and inspire in an imperfect world. We understand that being imperfect is ongoing process of overcoming with grace. It continues in the mantra of maintaining greatness and being a child of The Creator as we share from our hearts.

One of the final and most important practices to implement in order to inspire and influence is effective communication. Most influencers possess the ability to persuasively express thoughts and feelings with conviction and confidence. Too often, we lose the true sense of interaction and communication because of the constant stream of information flowing towards us at any moment. The technological advancements of our generation create barriers in some areas of communication. We can communicate with little to no emotion, connection, or love because we are (at times) desensitized to true communication. Influence or inspiration cannot exist without communicate on some level. Communication creates an environment for effectiveness in influence and inspiration. The Bible is a good reference because the stories build a foundation for the next generation, empowering each legacy with opportunity. The communication is so compelling that they are passed down to the next generation in order to inspire and influence. Bob Burg and John David Mann authored a influential book titled *"Go-Giver"* in which one of the characters is called "The Connector." His job was to influence and open doors for others, and this role is a great example of how you too can empower your legacy by opening doors for others. He was the connector; he knew because he'd been through the same struggles as other people around him. With that working knowledge he created relationships that were bigger than his individual purpose, and that is how we build legacy.

When I began writing this book, my sole mission was to inspire others to maintain greatness. As my vision became clear I realized that I had involved my mentors in the process. Great influencers do not mind uplifting someone because they understand the law of reciprocity. I was honored when Les Brown agreed to write the foreword for the book. Les Brown is one of the greatest influencers of our time. He talks about his story and being hungry in order to reach your dreams. The story still carries the same enthusiastic character even after hearing it years ago! He made it his mission to prepare by soaking up everything he could. He believed wholeheartedly that the opportunity would come, and he wanted to be ready. No one actually believed he was ready because they didn't see his efforts or how he took the time to inspire and motivate himself. One day, a DJ was on the radio but too inebriated to finish his show. Les was instructed to call and find another DJ instead, he knew that was his time to shine. He seized the moment and was able to go in the booth and finish the show. It was awesome and inspiring to hear this example, and it always will be. He was hungry and, to this day, it inspires me so much that I review that story often because the enthusiasm with which he shares it. It is truly one-of-a-kind –it lathered with his signature of inspiration, it is who he is. It's who we all are when we are hungry.

Influence and inspiration are similar to peanut butter and jelly. Individually they are good but together they are amazing. One can be an influencer and not inspire just as one can inspire without influencing action. It is important to consistently measure your influence and monitor your inspiration to ensure you are being effective in your interactions. Maintaining greatness creates a new level of influence and opportunities to influence others. So, we must be intentional in our actions and guided by the fruits of the spirit.

8

NIRVANA

"a state of happiness and peace."

NIRVANA

Greatness cannot be maintained if peace does not exist. I believe a small portion of the Buddhist philosophy lines up specifically with Christianity. The ultimate goal within both faiths is to live in peace. Peace must be a part of our everyday existence. The King James version of the bible mentions peace 429 times and love 310. When we embody unconditional love, peace will overtake us, allowing true nirvana to exist within. The simple definition for Nirvana is "a state of happiness and peace." It's a condition void of anything counterproductive to peace. It's like possessing a little piece of heaven. The third key in my first book, and arguably the most important key, is "agape," which is the same as unconditional love. Nirvana is draped with agape love, and only reached through tapping into our ability to love without boundaries and limitations.

Because nirvana is not commonly taught most people are unaware of how to attain it while others insist that it cannot be achieved. Nirvana does exist! People live free of sickness, anxiety and stress every single day. The state of nirvana can be totally embraced in the natural when we create environments of tranquility. Let's be transparent for a moment, based on things happening in the world today it can be hard to grasp the idea of nirvana. The truth lies within our ability to choose. Peace can be attained once a personal decision to occupy your mind with positivity begins. This is the part of your awareness that you alone must be accountable for. The power of choice is evident in the lives of some of the great shifters of our society. If we take a moment to evaluate the thought process of Jesus, Gandhi, Mother Teresa, or Martin Luther King Jr. (just to name a few), we will see how they looked beyond the realities of the world to create a personal nirvana. They lived by a code of unconditional love and faced opposition from the masses because of it. They stood boldly in their decision to create and share the idea or nirvana, regardless of what was going on. Each of them encouraged individuals to look beyond their current troubles to create a personal world of love, peace and happiness. They are remembered for their vigilance, standing and defending what they knew to be true.

Just like these examples teach us, separation from the way that the world perceives things will give a new perspective. The choice to walk in this perspective creates a buffer against the control of fear. Fear is what keeps people from living in agape love.

"There is no fear in love; but perfect love casts out fear"
John 4:18

Unfortunately, we live in a world constructed by fear, physically, mentally politically and beyond, fear has created a world where nearly everything is anti-peace, anti-God, and anti-nirvana. As long as mass killing, racial tension, abuse, and war exist, we will never have a complete or collective state of nirvana. But, we can make individual choices to create tranquility in our own lives. If we are going to blissfully engage in the state of nirvana, we have to master dealing with fear and love simultaneously. John 4:18 offers the best solution: "There is no fear in love; but perfect love casts out fear." When you live in agape; you are living an expectation of peace; when you embody and embrace the love that God has, you remain in a state of maintaining greatness.

Becoming personally accountable for our own forward movement requires grace and inner peace. If we all choose to embrace a state of nirvana, I believe that everything in the world can make a shift. God gives us an example of this in the promise to Solomon in Second Chronicles:

"If my people who are called by my name would humble themselves and pray, seek my face, and turn from their wicked ways, then I will hear from heaven, forgive their sins, and heal their land."

This passage displays yet another example of faith in action, covered by grace. If you practice maintaining greatness, grace is in the mist and covers all. In fact, God extends grace to all of us in every season and allows us to choose our path. Sadly, there are some who succumb to the world's lures and live in opposition to tranquility. Thankfully, we are able to decide at any time that nirvana is the state that we wish to continuously sustain.

CHOICES & APPLICATION

Once an individual chooses to create a personal state of nirvana, practical application steps maintain it. Nirvana requires giving, and this is perhaps one of the hardest first steps to take. In addition to giving up past ideas and thought patterns, one must selflessly give of all they possess. In the previous chapter I mentioned the mentoring journey with Richard Lee. I was able to demonstrate nirvana to him through agape love in an environment of tranquility. This environment was only attained through a deepened level of

> *"Nirvana is not unintentionally accomplished, one must make conscious efforts in every area of life to welcome it."*

spiritual meditation and prayer. This is the second step to creating nirvana, the bible instructs us to meditate in the bible both day and night in Psalms 1:2- *But his delight is in the law of the Lord, and in his law he meditates day and night.* The first two application steps pave the way for tranquil living to exist, while the ones that follow assist in preservation.

The most common thread within each chapter of maintain greatness is intentionality; with this in mind it is crucial to surround yourself with an environment more conducive to peace. Nirvana is not unintentionally accomplished. One must make conscious efforts in every area of life to welcome it. This is a personal step, for some it may include changing the music that you listen to, while aromatherapy may be the key for others. Peace involves individualized pieces but, in the end, the puzzle will look the same. Environmental nirvana is amplified through peaceful associations. Most of us become mirrors for the individuals we spend most of our time with. When we make intentional efforts to associate only with others who reflect similar efforts of nirvana the ability to uphold personal peace increases.

The final practical application step is to maintain a thankful heart. Thankfulness requires attention and attention yields appreciation. If we are operating in happiness and peace it becomes easy to be thankful. Nirvana is indeed possible but, it is a personal choice and necessary during the journey to maintaining greatness.

INTEGRITY

He who walks in integrity walks securely,
But he who perverts his ways will be found out.
Proverbs 10:9

INTEGRITY

Most of us have been trained to be someone other than the great individuals God created us to be. Maintaining greatness is a standard and responsibility of those individuals who have been exposed to their true purpose and identity. Integrity is a condition of the heart and often serves as our internal compass. Integrity is at the core of maintaining greatness because it is a part of the personal responsibility to know thy self. Most of the struggles to maintain greatness or walk in integrity arise because of a lack of self-awareness. Little things like telling "white lies" will not keep you from greatness, but those seemingly minute flaws must be addressed. It is important to constantly walk in your goals to consistently maintain integrity. If the goal is greatness, the actions along the journey should reflect a character of greatness. Integrity is often judged outwardly by others who interact with you at any given time. While this is an important part, it is not the most important aspect to integrity. Reputation is given to us, but integrity is what we give to others through actions, words and emotions. We will refer to this as personal integrity and define it as "staying true to yourself." Keep in mind that personal integrity can be interpreted in many ways based on the evaluator. Opinions often become the enemy to integrity and may cause confusion within. If we are unsure of who we are, the opinions of others will eventually obstruct our ability to walk in our truth.

An illustration of this may be Lebron James, who has been deemed as one of the greatest athletes of the 21st century. During the final edits of this book he became the trending topic of social media as he opened an academy for youth in elementary school. He made a personal decision to improve the community based on his personal experiences as a child and the integrity he has developed as an adult. While I cannot personally speak on the daily integrity he may practice with those closest to him, I can say that his mainstream examples of integrity and greatness have been commendable. Critics may offer invalid opinions of chastisement based on the dislike of his personal choices as an athlete. But while opinions may be great for debates, they are void when personal integrity is activated. When we stay true to our personal calling and passion, we create a personal path of integrity. This path can only be monitored or maintained on a personal level. Each of us have the personal responsibility to follow our passion and dream with integrity, just as Lebron James demonstrates.

Uncover, Operate, Execute

All of the trailblazers I've described in his book had flaws and may not have always operated in integrity. They were still considered great simply because they were courageous enough to uncover their purpose. They made personal commitments to be the greatest version of themselves- continuously. Integrity is rooted in your commitment to uncover what you were created to leave behind. It requires the conscious uncovering of purpose to become familiar with the space of integrity. Walking in integrity allows us to operate in greatness while executing the maintenance component. As we operate in the uncovered purpose there may be moments of subdued integrity. It is important to remember that this does not negate your purpose or truth. What makes greatness unique is the ability to be resilient and bounce back when things of integrity haven't been exercised to the fullest. Executable acts of integrity, driven by who you are and whose you are, can literally make you unstoppable.

The main component to integrity is knowledge of self. Thus, without proper identification of who you are, integrity cannot be maintained. Integrity paves a path of ethical living and implementation of choosing right over wrong. With very little effort we can identify an extensive list of individuals that have unfortunately had their embarrassing exploits of unethical behavior uncovered publicly. No matter the behavior or issue, they have one thing in common –the knowledge that

"No temptation has overtaken you but such as is common to man; and God is faithful, who will not allow you to be tempted beyond what you are able, but with the temptation will provide the way of escape also, so that you will be able to endure it."
1 Corinthians 10:13

God had to provide a way of escape. Most of them were able to bounce back because of the God-given way of escape. This is not in the form of running from problems or letting them consume us, it simply allows us to choose integrity and execute morality even in our imperfection.

David is a shining example for the do's and don'ts of integrity and ethics. He is often referred to as "a man after God's own heart." While it is undeniable that David did love God, it is also noted that he was not always ethical in his actions. One of the most popular bible stories of David is his infidelity with Bathsheba. She became pregnant as a result of their negligence and David sent her husband to his death in an attempt to cover his grave misdeed. He did not act with integrity. On another occasion, David had the opportunity to kill Saul in a cave, but decided to exercise restraint. The Bible stories of David emphasize more of his love for God and less of his indiscretions. That's where his true integrity was, despite any of his contradictory actions.

Integrity is what you find when you dig beneath the choices –the impulsive choices, the emotional choices, and the unconscious choices. Beyond the reaction, it's the residue that is left once everything has been stripped away. That's true integrity, and it will cause you to step forward and accept the greatness that you have as God's child. This brings about a understanding that He's faithful and just to forgive you and cleanse you from all unrighteousness. Integrity is not easy. Just like almost anything, it's a practice that you have to consciously perpetuate in order to maintain greatness. When you fall short in the area of integrity, repentance is required for redemption. God's forgiveness doesn't come with an expiration date. David was well aware of this fact and yet didn't abuse. We can learn to expose our hearts to God, and, the more we do that, the more his integrity will be reflected in our lives.

But now your kingdom shall not endure. The LORD has sought out for himself a man after his own heart, and the LORD has appointed him (David) as ruler over his people, because you have not kept what the LORD commanded you
1 Samuel 13:14

NOURISH

NOURISH

In the previous chapters when we discuss maintaining greatness, it refers to achievements of the past and the goals of the future. Traditional definitions of greatness focus on actions and achievements with little to no focus on nourishment. For example, if you were in need of a business to fix your roof, you may automatically link the years of service greatness. While years of service may be a good indicator of a trustworthy business, it does not guarantee greatness, nourishment does.

Nourishment refers to the steps needed to actually achieve and maintain greatness. Imagine getting the car of your dreams. Naturally you take excellent care of this car. You nourish the car by filling the tank and changing the oil. You even take it to get washed and waxed to ensure the exterior remains in a pristine state. The outside of the car and the parts under the hood are perfect but you never take time to clean the interior. In time you become content and no longer maintain the car of your dreams. You allow the gas tank to reach empty and oil changes are neglected. Eventually the car reaches an avoidable demise. Similarly, greatness is impossible without nourishing the spirit and physical body.

When we do not nourish our bodies, both inside and out, we willingly submit to the path of failure. Most of the legendary entertainers of or time have learned how to nourish their greatness. The old saying remains true "whatever we feed will grow and whatever we starve will die". Nourishment starts from the inside and manifests outwardly through our gifts.

Inner nourishment begins with spiritual maintenance. When we nourish our spirit, we strengthen the heart and positively affect the mind. This is a necessary practice for the development of discipline.

John 15 provides a clear picture of the benefits of nourishing our sprit. God instructs us to abide in Him to gain strength and produce. He further explains that we are limited without Him, just

"Abide in Me, and I in you. As the branch cannot bear fruit [a] of itself unless it abides in the vine, so neither can you unless you abide in Me. [5] I am the vine, you are the branches; he who abides in Me and I in him, he bears much fruit, for apart from Me you can do nothing."
John 15:4-5

as the branches cannot grow without the vine. When we make the personal choice to nurture our spirit, we make a conscious effort to bear fruit. Dr. Adrian Gentry sums it up in saying *"faith eats!"* Your faith needs to eat!

The faith eats movement focused on positive reprogramming related to health living. The eat, live, grow model begins with encouragement of appropriate nutrition, which leads to building good daily habits. The movement starts from the soil to create fertile ground. This is because nourishment at the root creates stronger foundations.

Spirituality

The things we listen to and actively pour into our minds adversely affect our spirit.

Let's revisit the example of the dream car. If the goal is longevity, then the owner will engage in simple steps to care for it by filling the tank with the appropriate gas. Likewise, nourishment for our spirit requires careful selection of fuel. We constantly pour in an abundance of bad music, poor television and tainted images into our spirit. We fill our tank with this gas effortlessly and daily because it is readily available. Truthfully, spiritual nourishment requires us to revisit our intentions. Again, if the goal is to maintain greatness, we must intentionally feed the spirit to produce a positive fruitful life from the inside out.

Part of the greatness we aim to maintain relies on our ability to nurture our physical bodies. The physical fuel refers to the foods we eat and the necessary movement needed to run effectively. Over the years the advent of the fast food and take-out industries has significantly changed our nutrition. Most people do not receive the balanced nutrition provided by farm-raised, home-cooked meals. Because so much has shifted, attempts to properly nourish our bodies have become a challenge. Our temples are supposed to be operational and healthy, but we are literally dying younger due to diseases, obesity, and mentally illness. Most of the conditions could possibly be avoided by simply eating better. This goes back to nourishing the spirit. If we properly focus on caring for our spirit we understand the responsibly affirmed in 1 Corinthians 10:31. Before partaking of any food or drink we must ask ourselves "*does this bring glory to God and nourish my*

> "*Whether, then, you eat or drink or whatever you do, do all to the glory of God.*"
> 1 Corinthians 10:31

temple?" The investment in your body in the form of proper nutrition is a necessary practice to build a bridge from the spirit to the physical body.

The human body is made up of 60% water and when we do not drink enough water, the effects can be detrimental to our health. Most weight gain can be combated with proper consumption of water. Focus can be sharpened and risk for major illness, such as stroke, can be significantly lowered. Water is a natural energy booster and purifier. Our bodies literally require water to release in the natural unassisted way. When we do not take the necessary steps to simply hydrate, we subconsciously send a message to our body. Unintentionally we place our body on the bottom of the priority list, giving it permission to malfunction. Maintaining greatness comes with a heightened responsibility to care for the physical body with the same level of emphasis we have placed on emotional well-being.

As we navigate through nourishing the spirit and physical body, it is equally as important to nourish our minds. Mental health is the most neglected of the three areas discussed simply because of stigmas and cultural barriers. Most generations are taught to rely solely on spirituality to combat mental struggles. This remedy gives little recognition to the fact that that the silent mental struggles, experienced on a regular basis, literally effect the physical body. On the other hand, if we are equipped nutritionally, the mental wear and tear will not shake the foundations of our physical health. Mental wellbeing is often a reflection of the environment and stimulants within it. Mental nourishment requires constant evaluation, reconstruction and release. For some, evaluation may include assistance from professionals, while for others it may mean simply changing the environment.

How can you be great if you are not operating at your fullest potential? While I cannot give the perfect prescription for spiritual, mental and physical nourishment, I can say that the most important step is move in the direction of health. The Bible tells us the things we should eat, but, from a simple and realistic standpoint, we can follow a few guidelines and be much healthier. Take color for instance, having an array of colors on our plates, especially green vegetables, can be a good starting point. Nourishment for the body can be as simple as taking a walk. So, you don't have to really get into all the depth of the nutrition industry to understand that you can make some significant changes to maximize and maintain greatness. We spend our younger years chasing wealth ,and success while trying to find our place in the world. More often than not we end up spending what we save on health related issues later in life. This is a vicious cycle that has to change and nourishment from a spiritual, mental and physical standpoint provide pivotal starting points. Just a little bit of nourishment goes a long way toward maintaining greatness.

"give and it shall be given unto you, good measure, pressed down, shaken together, running over shall man give unto your bosom."
Luke 6:38

11

GIVING

GIVING

Every success that I have ever obtained has been a product of giving. It is the key essential to maintaining greatness. The fact is, giving encompasses all of the other areas we have discussed during the journey to maintaining greatness. As an athlete I had to give my time to and practice my craft. I give unconditional love as a husband and father. As a coach, I give my energy and effort to every team or client. Everything we do requires giving on a conscious or subconscious level. During the process of giving we must be willing to stretch beyond the comfort zone. I challenge you to ask yourself how much you are willing to give while reading this chapter. Giving is a personal process and you have the power over.

Simple evaluation of the life of Jesus shows a demonstration that service is all about giving. The Bible reminds us of this in Mark 10:45 by saying "greatest among us is the servant to men." God gave us his only son so we may live more abundantly. Jesus gave his life and selflessly served as a sheppard of men. God gave us dominion and we were given the keys to the kingdom. He gave us an assignment to continue giving just as he gave and continues to give. Greatness is fortified when we give from the heart. All of the components of maintaining greatness involve the heart. This is because it is one of the greatest gifts that we must give in order to receive.

Luke 6:38 highlights the personal assignment to simply give. There is no set quantity to how much we must give or how often; the command is just to give. It must become an everyday habit that we implement on a conscious and subconscious level. Most of the

"give and it shall be given unto you, good measure, pressed down, shaken together, running over shall man give unto your bosom."
Luke 6:38

people you meet on a daily basis will never know your personal accomplishments or professional accolades. Daily conversations are not opened with a laundry list of our awards or educational achievements. Think about the first time you met someone you wanted to impress. You gave a different energy that invited them into your space. I'm almost certain you gave a smile or kind salutation. Now, imagine if you approached every situation in the same manner.

When you give from the heart it removes any expectation of reciprocity and allows you to focus on serving others. It is important to always keep in mind that you cannot receive what you do not give in some way. The law of reciprocity, karma and the laws of attraction all mirror the command in Luke chapter 6. This is because giving is a natural and unavoidable component of life. Every other component I have covered, until this point, involves reprograming of learned behaviors. Giving does not require any of this because we are wired for it. There are no pre-qualifications for giving, and there is no belief or religion that says you should not give. The more you give, you begin to uncover the natural wiring and operate in your greatness. Limitless living can only become a reality when giving is a daily practice. Functioning in this order allows us to focus on something outside of ourselves. The bottom line is, giving is FOR you but it is not ABOUT you. When you give, you create opportunities to operate in your gifts while maintaining greatness. It is a constant cycle of releasing good through service and receiving in ways you may have never known were even possible.

Take a moment and think about your best day this week. Now try and remember what you gave to that day for it to be so great. I am almost certain that the day was good for you because you made a choice to give your best energy to each second. You worked with your day instead of against it by withholding your best. When you hold on to something you have been commanded to give, it works against your faith. If you are committed to growing in your greatness, I challenge you to take daily inventory of your giving. When we give abundantly, we reap abundantly, just as when we give sparingly we reap sparingly. The greatness in you will be revealed and maintained through the extent at which you give.

John 3:16 is a verse so familiar that most could say it in their sleep. "For god so loved the world that he gave his only begotten son that whosoever believeth in him should not perish but have eternal life." God gave big to serve as an ultimate example of how much he loves giving.

One of the biggest mistakes I see as a metacognition expert is individuals who limit their receiving with limited giving. The opportunity to give is bigger than money and time. At any moment we can give our energy, love, attention or talents to others. Greatness

"12 very truly I tell you, whoever believes in me will do the works I have been doing, and they will do even greater things than these, because I am going to the father."
John 14:12

depends on your ability to dig deep and give in greater ways. The instructions to serve in greater ways are clear to us in John 14:12. Jesus was limitless in his giving and empowers us to choose giving through service in ways appropriate for our time. Giving is unlike any other component to maintaining greatness because you are in complete control.

Deuteronomy 15 talks about how we should give without a grudging heart; Proverbs 3 explains that we should not hold back good things from people who are deserving; Proverbs 21 talks about how righteous people give without holding back; Matthew 6 encourages us to give anonymously and promises the father's greater reward as a result; and Luke 6 talks about giving without expecting anything in return for your giving. There are countless scriptures in which God provides insight on giving. It is a prevailing theme demanding us to give of ourselves and the things we possess.

Everything prior to this chapter tells you how to maintain greatness while giving uncovers the action needed for actual implementation. Giving is undeniably the master key to maintain greatness and limitless living.

MARK 10:35-45

35)James and John, the two sons of Zebedee, *came up to Jesus, saying, "Teacher, we want You to do for us whatever we ask of You." 36 And He said to them, "What do you want Me to do for you?" 37 They said to Him, "Grant that we may sit, one on Your right and one on Your left, in Your glory." 38 But Jesus said to them, "You do not know what you are asking. Are you able to drink the cup that I drink, or to be baptized with the baptism with which I am baptized?" 39 They said to Him, "We are able." And Jesus said to them, "The cup that I drink you shall drink; and you shall be baptized with the baptism with which I am baptized. 40 But to sit on My right or on My left, this is not Mine to give; but it is for those for whom it has been prepared."

41 Hearing this, the ten began to feel indignant with James and John. 42 Calling them to Himself, Jesus *said to them, "You know that those who are recognized as rulers of the Gentiles lord it over them; and their great men exercise authority over them. 43 But it is not this way among you, but whoever wishes to become great among you shall be your servant; 44 and whoever wishes to be first among you shall be slave of all. 45 For even the Son of Man did not come to be served, but to serve, and to give His life a ransom for many."

12

Epilogue:

GREATNESS

GREATNESS

The idea for this book came to me during a lecture with a group entrepreneurs at my alma mater -Clemson University. One of the young men in the crowd asked a question that I have obviously never forgotten, *"What does it take to be great"?* Without hesitation the response flowed from my head and escaped with power and confidence *"You were born great."*

I explained to him that the true thing that plagues us all is maintaining our greatness. At some point in our pursuit of understanding we must arrive at the realization of our greatness. Your greatness was birthed the day you were born and minimized the day you decided you were less than great. We were created by a great God who gave his great son and showers us with great love. The man-made definition of greatness speaks of attaining greatness through power, brilliance and authority. But, as a child of God, greatness is a birthright. There is no denying that greatness is indeed in our DNA.

Mark 7 verse 13 warns of the traditions of man make the word of God ineffective. The passage outlines the logic that most of us have adopted as it relates to

"Thus you nullify the word of God by your tradition that you have handed down. And you do many things like that."
Mark 7:13

greatness. Most individuals live by the standard of greatness outlined by society and never reach a pinnacle of success.

Individuals in this group never feel that greatness has been achieved and therefore cannot be maintained. Their personal greatness is reduced by comparison to the accomplishments of others and life achievements are diminished to insignificant experiences. Life becomes a chore for individuals in this category because of they constantly chase greatness and lack knowledge of their birthright.

We all possess a natural desire to feel like we have done something great because greatness is within us. Labels and traditions assigned by man often yield vain efforts to satisfy the unquenchable quest for greatness. I want to take a moment to emphasize again that greatness is an expectation of the birthright. Therefore, the pursuit of greatness outside of your DNA is one of the greatest errors of man. When you are fully aware of your greatness, you begin to uncover your gifts. Uncovering your unique gifting unveils the zeal to maintain greatness. Fulfillment of life destiny is directly related to a clear understanding of the power within you to be great.

Evaluation

Along the path to discovering your gifting and maintaining your greatness, it is important to evaluate your intentions. Unevaluated intentions lead to ego-driven actions fuelled by recognition and power. It is imperative to identify ego-driven actions that do not line up with the intention to simply maintain greatness. I can recall countless examples of this from my time as a basketball coach. Some of the players on the team were driven by an ego that often overrode their intention to be an effective teammate. While their gifting may have been exceptional, their ability to serve with a team mindset was nonexistent. The players who craved constant recognition could easily be identified on the court. They were the ones who would aim for an impossible shot instead of passing the ball. Their ego depended on recognition to validate their gift. They could not serve the team because they were not fully aware of their misguided objective. Ego-driven intentions can often be identified in service and conquered through evaluation. Evaluation is the bridge of maintenance between service and receiving.

Service

Service to many leads to greatness. – John C. Maxwell

Do you believe that you are great? Are you willing to let your greatness shine in your gifting? Are you willing to serve? Now that you know what it takes to maintain greatness, I challenge you to walk in it. Walking in greatness requires service and service is an intimate matter of the heart. As you embrace your greatness, it is important to manage your gifts through service.

During my college days at Clemson University I completed 857 assist as athlete on the basketball team. My role was to obtain and pass the ball for someone else to score. On the court I was unstoppable because I knew what my gifting was and carried it out with all of my heart. Each pass was saturated in my intention to assist with the win. I knew what I could do and always kept the team in mind. While I cannot say that all eight hundred and fifty seven passes resulted in a score, I can say that I served with greatness. I was not responsible for anything outside of my managing my gift through service. This is the true essence of serving and greatness –using your gifts to help others achieve goals. Service to others is not a glamorous road, but it is the key trait of greatness.

When we serve from greatness, we stand at the door of limitless living and maintaining greatness allows us to enter in. Happiness is one of the elemental needs that can only be satisfied through operating in our God-given greatness. Most of us know our gifting and experience joy when operating in it. When we are happy, we enjoy the natural medicine of laughter and live in the abundance of our birthright. Most of the individuals we deem legendary have maintained their status through service. They were able to see that the continued growth of their gifting relied heavily on their ability to serve. They developed a new level of appreciation for their life when greatness was maintained. This level of greatness can be attained by anyone who chooses to manage their gifts.

The search for greatness outside of yourself ends when you began to operate in your gift. Recognizing your greatness and serving from the heart allows you to touch a place within that longs to be fulfilled. When we are unaware of our greatness it is almost impossible not to measure our success through the things we acquire. While money and other possessions are great, they cannot be solely responsible for satisfy the longing. Individuals who fill the longing with possessions often find themselves saddened by the search for greatness.

> "*It is the blessing of the* LORD *that makes rich,* *And He adds no sorrow to* *it*"
> Proverbs 10:22

Proverbs 10:22 reminds us of the benefits of the blessings of the lord –they add no sorrow. When I learned how to serve from my greatness, the blessings were abundant and regret free.

Serving in your gifting, with greatness, is the key to true fulfillment and limitless living. This requires faith, not only in God, but also in your calling. Greatness is not always visible to the eye, it is often an invisible calling carried out through service. You will never have to wonder how to become great once you learn how to manage what you already are. You are great, be legendary and maintain it!

MAINTAINING GREATNESS
Managing your gifts for limitless living

CHAPTER 1
M-Mastering the mind
Genesis1:24-31
Galatians 6:7-9
John 8:32
1 John 4:4
1 Corinthians 13:13
2Corithians 10:5

CHAPTER 2
A-Accountability
Luke 12:48
2 Corinthians 5:17
1 Corinthians 6:19
Philippians 4

CHAPTER 3
I-Intentional Living
Philippians 3:12-14
1 John 1:9
Isaiah 3:10
1 Corinthians 9:24-27

CHAPTER 4
N-Nurturing Relationships
Genesis 2:18
Proverbs 17:22
Ecclesiastes 4:9-12

CHAPTER 5
T-Thankfulness
1 Chronicles

CHAPTER 6
A-Association Quotient
Lamentations 3:22-24
Romans 12:2
1 Corinthians 14:33

CHAPTER 7
I-Influence
Galatians 5:22-23
Psalm 73:6

CHAPTER 8
N-Nirvana
John 4:18
2 Chronicles7:14
Psalm 1:2

CHAPTER 9
I-Integrity
Proverbs 10:9
1 Corinthians 10:13
1Samuel 13:14

CHAPTER 10
N-Nourishment
John 15:4-5
1Corinthians 10:31

CHAPTER 11
G-Giving
Luke 6:38
John 3:16
Deuteronomy 15
Proverbs 3,21
Matthew 6
Mark 10:35-45

Epilogue
Greatness
Mark 7:13
Proverbs :10:22

ABOUT THE AUTHOR

Grayson Marshall, Jr., a Washington, D.C. native, is a kingdom minded servant, inspirational leader, gifted keynote speaker, and entrepreneur. He has traveled around the globe and inspired tens of thousands of people to live their lives to the fullest.

Grayson is an accomplished athlete and coach. He was a five-time high school basketball Coach of the Year; was inducted into the St. John's College High School Hall of Fame, and was inducted into the Clemson University Sports Hall of Fame. Clemson University recently named him an ACC Basketball Legend. Grayson still holds every assist record in the university's history. He is a graduate of Clemson University and became a Certified Life Coach.

Grayson has the unique talent of "Getting you to Believe in you." He is called "The Metacognition Expert," because the lasting application to make the successful shift is all in the way you think. He utilizes tools and techniques to help people change their outlook on life and identify their passion. Grayson's energy and enthusiasm are contagious, which is why so many seek him out to address and inspire their organizations, no matter what the size.

Made in the USA
Columbia, SC
20 November 2018